Encounters with
AUSTRALIAN BIRDS

Finding inspiration in Australia's amazing birdlife

Stephanie Jackson

DEDICATION

To my best mate Andrew, who's finally learnt
to distinguish a cormorant from a penguin
and who, despite my occasional bouts of nagging,
still thinks that I'm the best bird in his life.

Published in 2023 by Reed New Holland Publishers
Sydney

Level 1, 178 Fox Valley Road, Wahroonga, NSW 2076, Australia

newhollandpublishers.com

Copyright © 2023 Reed New Holland Publishers
Copyright © 2023 in text and photos: Stephanie Jackson

A record of this book is held at the National Library of Australia.

ISBN 978 1 92554 695 8

Managing Director: Fiona Schultz
Publisher and Project Editor: Simon Papps
Designer: Andrew Davies
Production Director: Arlene Gippert
Printed in China

10 9 8 7 6 5 4 3 2 1

OTHER TITLES BY REED NEW HOLLAND INCLUDE:

Australian Wildlife On Your Doorstep, Second Edition
Stephanie Jackson
ISBN 978 1 92107 320 5

Slater Field Guide to Australian Birds. Second Edition
Peter Slater, Pat Slater and Raoul Slater
ISBN 978 1 87706 963 5

Australian Birds In Pictures
Matthew Jones and Duade Paton
ISBN 978 1 92554 634 7

Parrot Conservation
Rosemary Low
ISBN 978 1 92554 646 0

A First Book of Australian Backyard Wildlife Sounds (book with speaker)
Fred van Gessel
ISBN 978 1 92554 685 9

A First Book of Beautiful Bird Songs (book with speaker)
Fred van Gessel
ISBN 978 1 92554 677 4

For details of these books and hundreds of other Natural History titles see newhollandpublishers.com and follow ReedNewHolland on Facebook

Keep up with Reed New Holland Publishers:

 NewHollandPublishers

 @newhollandpublishers

Barking Owl.

Contents

Introduction

"Why do you want to go to the outback, dear?" my mother once enquired as I revealed the itinerary for my latest Australian adventure. "There's nothing there other than deserts and desolate plains," she added as though she was as familiar with the region as a flea might be with every feature of a mangy mongrel's hairy hide. I tactfully camouflaged any hint of disagreement with a subtle smile but beneath my calm exterior I was as angry as a gecko on a meat ants' nest. My simmering frustration was tempered by sympathy for a woman who had never dared to venture beyond her comfort zone of suburbia and who had no concept of the incredible diversity and beauty of the vast Australian outback, so rather than trigger an argument I simply stifled my emotions, gave my mother a hug and waved goodbye as I began my journey.

It is an indisputable fact that much of the outback is cloaked with extensive deserts and vast treeless plains but it's also a place of stunning and unexpected splendour where landscapes are either daubed with lakes, severed by streams and rivers, carpeted with wildflowers, or dominated by woodlands. This vast inland region is home to many of Australia's unique and beautiful wild creatures and it's here and in the forests and woodlands of less arid regions of the continent that I encountered the more than 50 species of birds that are featured in this book.

I have aimed to provide an abundance of facts regarding the habitats and physical and behavioural characteristics of each species and also relate the often humorous stories of face-to-face encounters with some of the country's most awe-inspiring birds – from the majestic Wedge-tailed Eagle and the elegant dancing Brolga to the diminutive yet charismatic Red-capped Robin and the endangered Superb Parrot that's as beautiful as its name suggests. I never set out to search for a specific species or to discover the rarest of birds, for I'm as enthralled by encounters with familiar characters such as Australian Brush-turkeys and Galahs as I am by a few moments spent in the presence of more elusive species such as Superb Lyrebirds and Squatter Pigeons.

Unlike the most dedicated of ornithologists and birders I don't methodically record every detail of every sighting. I rely entirely on my photographs and on my pin-sharp memory and I'm not averse to bragging that I can readily recall the exact moment and the exact place where I spotted each species that's honoured me with even a fleeting glimpse of its presence, for every avian encounter has been an unforgettable experience.

I've had endless opportunities not only to admire the beauty of birds but also to take a glimpse into their daily lives. I've watched their comings and goings and their interactions with one

Spotted Bowerbird landing at an outback waterhole.

another and with the natural environment, and I've listened to their varied twittering, chirping and screeching calls and to their melodious songs that hold me spellbound with wonder far longer than Pavarotti or Elvis could even do.

One of the primary rules of birdwatching is to be as quiet as possible but I've often found that once a bird has spotted me, providing I make no sudden movements and no excessively loud noises, it demonstrates as much concern about my presence as a comatose cockroach might show to a colony of bacteria partying in a mould-cloaked carpet.

I'm not completely antisocial but I have to admit that at times I struggle to involve myself in conversations with other human beings, but I'm never reluctant to commence a one-sided debate with my feathered friends and I chatter enthusiastically to every bird I meet, greeting each as though it was the most intimate of mates.

"Don't worry about me old fella. I'll be quieter than a swarm of caterpillars in a cabbage patch and I won't disturb your sleep," I whispered to a Barking Owl as it scowled down from its arboreal retreat and acknowledged my presence with a subtle wink of one of its large golden eyes. I had plenty to say to a flock of Superb Fairy-wrens too. "Don't mind me! Just make yourself at home," I muttered sarcastically as the birds invited themselves into my tent, explored the interior of my sleeping bag and sampled a sandwich that I'd left unattended. "I'd have baked a cake if I'd known you were coming to visit my humble abode," I added as they scurried around my feet before saying farewell with joyous twittering that made me sad to see them go.

Anyone who's in the vicinity when I'm conversing with my avian mates might assume that I'm a few sheep short of a flock or have little more intelligence than a greasy dish sponge but the birds generally seem unperturbed by my muted mutterings. Whether whispering words of admiration or sitting in silence I'm in awe of them all – the arrogant and haughty ones that are perpetually preening their feathers, the inquisitive birds that can't resist the urge to explore the interior of my campervan or tent, the aggressive species with dominating personalities and others that are subservient, the large and the small, from sparrows to eagles, each and every one provides me with a feast of pleasure.

I watch the varied antics of birds with the frivolous thought that perhaps they are performing merely to entertain me or are simply having fun but there's a logical reason behind every avian activity and everything that birds do relates to the search for food, for a mate, or for territory, with their ultimate goal being to procreate and thus ensure the survival of their species. I do my best to ensure that I have no detrimental impact on their lives or on the natural environment that is their home, for birds, like every creature that crawls, wriggles, strolls, or flutters across the landscape, are an integral and vital component of the complex web of life on Earth that is essential not only for wildlife but also for the long-term survival of the human race.

While some of the birds featured in this book inhabit only arid inland regions of the continent, others have less fastidious requirements and can be found not only in outback regions or in forests but also in urban areas. I hope that, when reading of my often humorous encounters with birds, you'll say, with a touch of envy, "I wish I'd seen that" and be inspired to head to the great outdoors to enjoy your own unique and personal encounters with the many amazing and awe-inspiring birds that call Australia home.

The Art of Birdwatching

Many people, when they're out in the Australian bush, are as unaware of the infinite details of the world around them as a decapitated glove puppet might be of its companions in a toy box. With loud and chattering voices and heavy footsteps they stomp along trails that meander through forests and notice little more than the confusion of trees that are the most prominent vegetation. Others who venture into the outback may see nothing more than the vast canvas of arid plains that are inhabited by mobs of kangaroos and flocks of Emus that are almost impossible to miss. They remain oblivious to the low shrubs, tufts of spiny grass and rocky outcrops that are an integral part of the natural habitat of an amazing array of birds and other wild creatures and, with their eyes and minds closed to the wonders of the natural world, they are unlikely to see anything that's even a tad more lively than the roadside corpse of a kangaroo.

"I've done this trail. I've done that track. I've been to Oodnawoopwoop and back," some travellers vociferously boast as they list their accomplishments and although they've visited many wonderful places what did they really see if every destination was nothing more than another name to tick off a bucket list? The answer is that, like a woman I met in the Queensland outback town of Bedourie, they've seen nothing at all.

This amiable stranger warned me that I was in for a very tedious journey as I headed south towards the iconic Queensland town of Birdsville with my intention being to then follow the Strzelecki Track that snakes through northern South Australia. "There's absolutely nothing to see out there, just miles and miles of barren and dusty plains," she insisted. "Let your husband do the boring job of driving and you can do what I did and sleep or read a book to pass the time," she added as I silently cringed at her comments. I've always assumed that anyone who could see nothing of interest along such a route would either have to be as blind as a block of granite or have a passion for the outback that would rival my enthusiasm for a wet weekend in a broom cupboard, but I responded with nothing more than a polite smile as I kept my thoughts to myself and my foot well clear of my mouth.

I've rarely seen any fragment of the outback that presents no visual appeal in some way but perhaps that's just because I'm easy to please or have the ability to spot the most meagre hint of natural beauty. As I eventually dawdled along the route that my fleeting acquaintance regarded as being devoid of any interesting features I gazed in wonder at the gaudy wildflowers that freckled rolling sand dunes. I watched Wedge-tailed Eagles dining on the bloodied carcass of a kangaroo and spotted a scrawny Dingo trudging lethargically across the plains that embraced a diminutive stream. Only someone who was dozing as soundly as Rip Van Winkle could have failed to see this picturesque scene where water, which seeps from the ground even during the most heavy-handed of droughts, has created a sanctuary for many species of birds. Within only a few minutes of my arrival at the water's edge I'd spotted Little Corellas, Galahs, Red-rumped Parrots, Whistling Kites and Zebra Finches among the surrounding vegetation of this isolated and welcoming oasis. And with Australian Pelicans, White-necked Herons, Yellow-billed Spoonbills and Black-fronted Dotterels taking their turn to parade along the banks of the creek and through its shallow waters I was in no hurry to leave.

The skills you'll need

Fortunately birdwatching doesn't require any expensive equipment, although a pair of binoculars certainly comes in handy. Everything that's required to see some of the world's most beautiful creatures costs no more than a breath of fresh air. At the top of the list of essential requirements is an abundance of time blended with a hefty serving of patience.

The basic skills for successful birdwatching can be mastered by anyone with a tad more intelligence than a fossilised amoeba and it's an ability to remain still and silent for prolonged periods of time that will guarantee the optimum number of awe-inspiring encounters with birds. It's also essential to have good observational skills and to be aware of every intimate detail of the

Dunn's Swamp and the forests of Wollemi National Park, New South Wales, hold a great diversity of birds.

environment and of everything that's going on in the world around you. A minute movement of the foliage of trees, shrubs or grasses may be nothing more than a murmuring breeze passing by but it might be a bird discreetly rummaging for seeds, for insect prey or for fragments of vegetation for the construction of a nest.

Unless you're as deaf as a swarm of desiccated dung beetles you'll also need to hone your auditory skills to ensure that you're alert to every subtle sound of the bush. The fluttering of wings and subdued twittering and chirping among congested foliage, the near-silent rustling of leaves, scratching sounds among grasses and stones that are scattered across an outback landscape or debris strewn across a forest floor could all be indications that a bird is in the vicinity.

If you're hoping to see a specific species you'll have the best chance of a successful sighting if you're armed with some knowledge of your quarry's favoured habitat and food sources and can recognise its unique calls. You'll definitely be on the winning track if you also have some idea of where it might be at a specific time of the day when its routine is to feed, drink, bathe or roost, but if you have no more knowledge of avian lives than a garden gnome has of the plants that surround it don't despair. You can simply wait and see whatever birds come your way and there's always the chance, if you've found a location that birds find irresistible, that when a completely unexpected or unfamiliar bird strolls or flutters into view you'll be as excited as the legendary King Midas when he first discovered that everything he touched turned to gold.

In the outback, particularly during a drought when water is as scarce as a scarecrow's tears, any source of water, from a diminutive stream to the remnants of a rapidly evaporating muddy puddle, will attract birds. Immense flocks and solitary birds will often arrive to quench their thirst

The shallow water of the Ross River near Alice Springs attracts many species of birds.

at dawn or late in the afternoon and while it's the early bird that gets the worm it's often the early birdwatcher who's up and about at the crack of dawn who has the best chance of seeing the greatest number of bird species.

If you're camping in the outback or in the heart of a forest and have set up your temporary home beside water you won't have far to go to find the perfect spot to wait for some avian action to begin. If there are flowering trees nearby that will lure honeyeaters, swathes of grasses with seed heads that beckon with the offer of a free snack, or other natural food sources that birds will find irresistible then you might not have long to wait.

To optimise your chances of seeing more than a fleeting glimpse of a bird or two conceal yourself among jumbled boulders or tall grasses or among the darkest shadows and the dense foliage of whatever vegetation is available to make yourself as inconspicuous as a white dove in a flock of Sulphur-crested Cockatoos. If you remain almost as motionless as a moss-covered boulder then birds will probably regard you as nothing more than an insignificant and harmless component of the landscape. When you finally need to move, as your limbs or feet begin to ache or you need to follow a bird that's heading elsewhere, move slowly and stealthily, one almost imperceptible and cautious step at a time.

Clothes

Many dedicated birdwatchers wouldn't be seen without their drab camouflage clothing and would react with horror at a mere glimpse of the brightly coloured attire that I generally wear. I usually tone down my wardrobe when I'm hoping to see birds in their natural environment however and, dressed in muted shades of brown and green, I blend into the landscape and improve my chances of going unnoticed by the birds but the truth is that there's very little that escapes their attention. With their highly developed eyesight they have the ability to see a far great range of colours than we mere humans. In addition to the familiar rainbow of colours that are visible to our eyes they can also see parts of the ultraviolet spectrum and this enables them to see the subtle differences between similar shades of colour and thus be able to locate insects and other prey that, as far as humans are concerned, are so perfectly camouflaged within their natural environment that they are almost invisible.

When you're selecting the most appropriate clothing to wear ensure that you toss aside anything white, for birds often regard white as a sign of danger. It's not merely the colour of clothing that's of importance however. Remember, this is birdwatching we're talking about, so there's no need to try to impress anyone by wearing the most fashionable and expensive garb. It's far more important to wear clothes that are comfortable and that are the most practical for the situation – and the birds won't give a razoo if you appear as unattractive as a swarm of maggots in a wet paper bag.

In hot weather shorts and a short-sleeved shirt might seem to be the obvious choice of attire but such clothing is not always the most appropriate. Trousers and a long-sleeved shirt made from a cool and lightweight fabric will not only provide a barrier to mosquitos and stinging insects but will also protect your skin from the sun and from scratches inflicted by sharp twigs and the mayhem of spiny plants that thrive in many outback regions.

The outback can be very cold in the winter months with temperatures often plummeting to below zero, particularly at dawn and dusk when you might be out and about in your search for birds. Wearing several layers of relatively thin clothing rather than one or two thick and bulky garments is the best option to ensure that you stay warm and cosy. You can then remove a layer as you warm up during a walk through the bush and put it back on again when you're standing still and watching your quarry for a prolonged period of time and feeling rather cool in a period of inactivity.

Every item of clothing should be loose enough to be comfortable and allow easy movement, yet not so loose that it easily becomes hooked on protruding twigs or branches that you might wander past – and certainly not so loose that the fabric flaps around in the gentlest of breezes and thus alerts birds to your presence.

You'll discover many species of birds in and around outback towns, in popular camping sites and in other places that are easily accessible to every traveller, but if you want to escape from the madding crowd and head into areas where there is no hint of human civilisation and plan to combine some bush walking with your birdwatching adventure, make sure that you're well-prepared for the excursion.

The number one requirement for walking in the bush is a pair of sturdy boots that provide good ankle support and have soles with good grip to ensure that you don't lose your footing on wet and slippery ground or when you're clambering across rocky surfaces. If you've purchased new boots make sure that you wear them in for a while before you head out on your jaunt. The last thing you'll want is new boots that are uncomfortable, that cause painful chafing and blisters and that squeak and thus inform every bird in the vicinity that you're coming its way.

You might not be setting out on a long and demanding expedition but even on a relatively short hike there are several things you should do before your departure to ensure that your day doesn't become a memorable one for all the wrong reasons. Don't forget the old slip, slop, slap jingle – slip on a shirt (preferably a long-sleeved one), slop on the sunscreen and slap on a hat. Even on a winter's day, with intense sunlight beaming down from cloudless skies, it's a wise idea to protect yourself from the risk of sunburn and skin cancer.

Equipment

You don't need to burden yourself with a load that would make even an Olympic weightlifter groan under the strain but some basic items make life just a little bit easier and more comfortable. Start with a small and lightweight backpack in which you can carry a waterproof jacket if there's even a vague hint that wet weather may be on the way and some warm clothing that might be needed if you expect to be outdoors as a winter's day draws to a close. You'll need your binoculars of course, as well as a notebook and pen to record your sightings. Toss in some energy-rich snacks and a flask of water to sustain you in case you walk further than you expected to in pursuit of a bird and, as a safety precaution, carry a torch or a headlight so you can find you way back to your vehicle or camping area if night descends over the landscape while you're still on a deserted walking trail.

When you begin your walk don't forget to turn your phone off so it doesn't ring with some blaring tune that will scare away every creature within cooee and remember that if you need to use your phone in an emergency you might be rudely reminded that, in many outback areas, the chance of being able to get a signal is on a par with the probability that you'll spot a white wallaby wearing wellies.

Even experienced bushwalkers occasionally become lost in the outback, sometimes with fatal consequences and I have to admit that on a few occasions I've become disoriented and, in a moment of panic, have lost my way. It's all very well to offer the advice that you should stay on a well-defined track but birds refuse to adhere to manmade routes and following them is almost

Dawn is the best time to see the birds of the outback that are invariably drawn to water.

guaranteed to lead you away from the straight and narrow path every now and then. Keeping your eye on the bird rather than on the trail means that sometimes you might find yourself in a predicament where one bit of bushland looks much the same as a thousand others and the trail that you were following is suddenly nowhere to be seen.

Before you detour from a defined track make a mental note of where the sun is in relation to the path, to your campsite or to where you parked your vehicle. Is it directly behind you, ahead of you, or to one side? That simple observation will make it far easier to gain your bearings and return to a safe and familiar location.

As you wander beyond a marked trail in search of an elusive bird make some marks on the ground to enable you to retrace your steps. Place a stone along your route every now and then or some sticks forming an arrow that points in the direction from which you came and make a point of remembering any unusual features that you wander past, such as unique rock formations or strangely shaped logs that you've had to step over.

When you've eventually discovered the birds that you'd hoped to see, birds that made you gasp in awe at their beauty and perhaps at their curious antics, don't forget to whisper a sincere thanks to them for the entertainment that they have freely provided.

Outback wildflowers that bloom after rain attract insects that, in turn, attract birds.

The most fanatical of birdwatchers might react with horror at any suggestion that a birdwatcher should make even a muted sound when in the hallowed presence of birds, let alone talk to these wild creatures, but when I've spent some quiet time with my feathered friends they eventually realise that I pose no threat whatsoever and a little polite and murmured conversation never scares them away. It simply makes every encounter a more memorable experience between a wild creature and a human who, for a brief moment of time, share the same corner of the world.

Outback Travel Tips

Before you pack your car, caravan, camper trailer or motorhome with everything you think you'll need for an adventure take some time to consider exactly where your journey will take you. Every road trip, even one to the local supermarket, involves some risks but if you're heading into the outback don't forget that travel in remote and arid regions comes with its own inherent dangers, some of which can be life-threatening.

A blend of poor road conditions, scorching summer temperatures and a lack of communications can create a recipe for disaster, particularly for travellers who are unprepared for the conditions that they'll encounter. If you intend to visit some of the most remote corners of inland Australia you'll need to remember that you're definitely not as invincible as a comic-book superhero.

The Grim Reaper is always waiting in the wings for the arrival of another foolhardy and ill-prepared traveller so, unless you're impatient to discover if there really is an afterlife, take the

Always take extreme care and use common sense when crossing a flooded outback road.

time to ensure that you're adequately prepared for every eventuality that you might face in the areas where your journey might ultimately lead you. The number one priority is to have a well-maintained vehicle that's suitable for the specific road conditions that you'll encounter. If you'll be driving only on bitumen roads your journey will be as easy as winning a game of tiddlywinks with a geriatric teddy bear but if you plan to travel off the beaten track and hope to see the birds that inhabit areas where unsealed roads are rough and rocky or merely narrow tracks that meander through deep sand, you'll need a vehicle, preferably a four-wheel drive with high ground clearance, that can traverse the terrain and get you safely to your destination.

Travelling in the outback is as much about how you drive as what you drive however. During my more than three decades of outback travel I've been to some extremely remote places via some incredibly rugged tracks. My chariot has often been a 1973 Citroen that trundles along with only the power of a two-cylinder 600cc engine but it's been my ability to assess the road conditions, to know the limitations of my vehicle and to travel at a speed that's appropriate for the terrain that have got me everywhere I've wanted to go.

Long distances separate many of the towns of the outback and although you might be impatient to reach your destination try to keep your speed down, particularly if you're travelling on unsealed roads. I'm not suggesting that you confine yourself to a speed that's little faster than that of a pedal car with square wheels but back off on the throttle a bit. You'll not only coax better fuel economy from your vehicle but you'll also be able to take the time to appreciate the region's stunning landscapes, to see unique outback flora and to improve your chances of finding some idyllic birdwatching locations.

Many outback roads are unfenced so you'll need to keep your eyes peeled for mobs of kangaroos, flocks of emus, herds of sheep and cattle and feral animals such as pigs and donkeys that may unpredictably rush across your path. If you're travelling at a relatively slow speed you'll have a far greater chance of seeing any hint of danger and be able to take evasive action to avoid a collision that might cause significant damage to your vehicle and bring your journey to a premature conclusion.

Slow and steady is definitely the way to go when you're approaching cattle grids too as slamming your tyres against the first steel bar of a grid and pounding, at high speed, into the gaping potholes that are often at the approach to a grid can cause serious damage to your vehicle's tyres.

When you're rolling along one of the narrow single-lane bitumen roads that crisscross the outback there's a good chance that, in addition to wandering animals, you'll also encounter an oncoming vehicle every now and then and although it may sound as though I'm nagging I have to say, once again, don't attempt to emulate the speed of a sinner fleeing from the demons of Hades or you might live to regret it.

The correct etiquette when travelling on narrow roads is to move over as far as possible to

Many outback roads, such as this one near Oodnadatta, South Australia, can become impassable after rain.

allow another vehicle to pass safely and as you jolt off the bitumen reduce your speed as you hit the road's often rough or sandy shoulder to ensure that you minimise the risk of losing control of your vehicle. You'll perhaps curse the outback's roads as a cloud of dust engulfs you and stones chatter against the bodywork of your vehicle but if you've done the right thing and reduced your speed and pulled as far off the narrow road as you can you should avoid any damage to your windscreen.

Narrow roads are certainly not the place where you want to meet a road train. These iconic outback trucks, towing three or more trailers, are around 53 metres in length and weigh up to 120 tonnes, so if you see one looming on the horizon or approaching from behind keep as far to the left as you can and let the driver and his great beast have all the room they need to pass in safety. The bloke behind the wheel of a big rig is simply doing his job and has a schedule to maintain and will thank you for your courtesy with a friendly wave rather than an unheard curse that he reserves for those inconsiderate drivers who make his job more stressful than it already is.

If you come across drovers with a mob of cattle out on the long paddock don't forget that, although you're on holiday, these men and women are actually working. They won't appreciate a demonstration of your impatience if, with a blaring horn, you plough through their herd of cattle that are dawdling along the road and send the panicked animals gallivanting off in every direction. Stop and wait for the drovers to move their livestock aside and wave you through, then drive slowly past the cattle as they grudgingly move out of your way at their own steady pace rather

It's easy to get lost on the tracks that meander through the Northern Territory's East MacDonnell Ranges.

than becoming as agitated as a gaggle of jitterbugging jellyfish with their tentacles in a tangle. Once again, your consideration and courtesy will be appreciated – and how much time did you really waste?

Some 'experts' will tell you that speed is essential when you're travelling along an unsealed road that has a severely corrugated surface. Believe me, that's nothing more than a myth that only those who have never driven in such conditions would accept as being entirely truthful, for there's no hard and fast rule that dictates the optimum speed to travel across the roughest of roads. In some situations a moderate speed can certainly improve the ride but at times, when the corrugations are most severe, travelling at a slow pace is the only option. It's a matter of modifying your speed to suit the conditions, for not all corrugations are created equal. You'll need to find a speed that's not so fast that your vehicle becomes uncontrollable as you shake, rattle and roll around every bend in the road and yet not so slow that you're dawdling along at a speed rivalling that of a rat swimming through a vat of treacle. It's sometimes hard to find a comfortable medium but on rough roads, as on all roads in the outback, safety rather than speed should always be foremost in your mind.

If your route will take you along treacherously sandy tracks or down rugged and rocky trails a generous dose of common sense and a modicum of caution will certainly come in handy. One important rule is that if you encounter difficult conditions that make you question whether you can safely progress any further, err on the side of caution and don't attempt to push on in an act of bravado. Play it safe and look for an alternative route or turn around and, if possible, go back the way you came.

The chances are that, at some stage of an outback journey, you'll be faced with a creek crossing, particularly if you're travelling off the beaten track or in some national parks where roads bear no resemblance to highways. At first glance the water across the road might appear to pose as little threat as a gravy-soaked Yorkshire pudding but don't be fooled. It might hide a vehicle-swallowing chasm where floodwaters have ripped away the road's surface and there might be submerged rocks, logs or other hidden obstacles, so proceed with caution and, if possible, wade through the water to check for any submerged obstacles before you attempt to drive through it. Keep well away from fast-flowing floodwaters however and if the water is too strong to safely walk through then it's probably too strong to drive through as well.

Even relatively shallow water can pose a risk by splashing up over a vehicle's engine so before you get your tyres wet you should not only be aware of the depth of the water but should also know the location of your vehicle's air intake and of its most vulnerable electronic components. If these get wet or water is sucked into the engine your vehicle will gurgle and splutter to a halt in the middle of the creek, leaving you feeling as happy about the immediate future as a mafia informant who's just learnt that he's next in line for a concrete overcoat.

If you've carefully assessed the situation and decided that it's safe to drive through the water use a low gear and drive at a speed that's adequate to create a bow wave in front of your vehicle. This will create a pocket of air under the bonnet that will help to prevent water from getting into the engine bay.

Some outback roads are little more than sandy tracks and unless you drive in the appropriate way there's a good chance that your progress on such terrain will be slow. If the sand is deep and soft the best option, if you're in a four-wheel drive vehicle, is to engage low range, but the most important tactic is to reduce the air pressure in your vehicle's tyres, something that can make the difference between getting through the sand or getting hopelessly bogged. If the steering feels heavy and your vehicle is struggling to plough through the sand its tyres are over-inflated and you'll need to reduce the pressure so that the vehicle is floating on top of the sand rather than pushing its way through it. Of course, if you deflate your tyres you'll need a tyre pressure gauge and also a compressor to reinflate your tyres once you're out of the sand and back on terra much firma.

Drive at a relatively slow speed that allows you to maintain forward movement. Follow the tracks of other vehicles that have already compacted the sand and try not to make any sharp turns or sudden manoeuvres that will encourage the vehicle's tyres to dig into the sand and if you have to stop while traversing a sandy track come to a standstill, if possible, on level ground or preferably with your vehicle pointing down hill to minimise the likelihood of getting bogged when you're ready to head on your way once again.

It's always wise to keep an eye on the sky and to regularly check the weather forecast, for even light rain can transform a dusty outback road into a quagmire in little more time than it takes for a mischief of mice to fight their way out of a wet paper bag.

When travelling on a muddy unsealed road drive on the crest of the road if possible and although you'll need to keep up enough speed to keep moving forward, don't go so fast that you'll risk losing control of your vehicle. The vision of sliding off the road and into a ditch oozing with mud is as appealing as the thought of holding a Christmas party in a shoebox and if you find yourself in such a situation you certainly won't be going anywhere in a hurry.

If wet weather sees you become stranded in some sleepy little town for several days you'll probably feel a little frustrated, but it will be nothing compared to a situation where impassable roads have brought your journey to a slithering halt and you become trapped in the bush. If you do get stuck – don't panic. You won't be the first person to land yourself in trouble in the outback.

The low vegetation that lines the road near Yowah, Queensland, is the habitat of many species of birds.

Ensure you're well prepared if you intend to visit a remote area such as Chambers Gorge, South Australia.

If you've done the right things and ensured that you have enough food and water to last for a few days you'll survive the crisis and live to tell the tale and you're sure to learn something valuable.

In many parts of the outback, particularly once any hint of civilisation has vanished beyond the horizon, you'll have as much chance of getting a signal on your mobile phone as you would have of swatting a fly with an egg whisk. That means that if your vehicle breaks down, if you become bogged or if any other disaster occurs you won't be able to call for assistance unless you have a satellite phone or some other advance form of communication.

Before you head off the beaten track, ask locals for information about current road conditions, let someone know where you're heading and when you expect to arrive and carry a personal locator beacon. Then there's a good chance that in the event of an accident the cavalry will come rushing to your rescue. Don't forget that if disaster does strike you should stay with your car as it's far easier for those searching to locate a vehicle than to find a person wandering through the bush.

If you avoid summer days when the weather is hot enough to make even Beelzebub feel a little hot under the collar, are well prepared for your adventure and travel with common sense and caution as your companions all should be well and when Mother Nature introduces you to the birds that call the outback home you'll be as happy as a caterpillar in a cabbage patch.

BIRDS OF PREY

Barking Owl

Ninox connivens

At night, whether I'm at home or camping in the bush, I sleep so soundly that I'm generally oblivious to the varied sounds that drift across the landscape when nocturnal creatures are out and about.

During a visit to the Coongie Lakes National Park, which lies in a remote corner of northern South Australia, I was once again well away in the land of nod and unaware of the stealthy activities of Barking Owls that were enthusiastically hunting their prey. At the first hint of daybreak I slithered out of my sleeping bag and with all thoughts of breakfast forfeited in my eagerness to explore this wild and wonderful corner of the world it was I who was out and about and on the prowl as the sun crept lazily across the horizon.

With time and patience as my allies I discovered my prey by luck rather than by any skills of observation. Gnawing pangs of hunger were instantly forgotten when my eyes met the gaze of a Barking Owl that was dozing in a hollow in an ancient eucalyptus tree on the banks of the iconic Cooper Creek that was merely a few metres from my tent.

"Don't worry about me mate. I won't disturb you," I whispered as it scowled down from its retreat and acknowledged my presence with a subtle wink of one of its large golden eyes, an action that has earned this beautiful bird the alternative name of 'Winking Owl.'

Barking Owls are skilful predators that snatch their prey from the ground, from trees, from vegetation and from the surface of water. Any creatures that they can carry in their long talons are fair game, including native marsupials such as possums and sugar gliders in addition to rabbits, rodents, reptiles, insects, birds as large as magpies and even bats that they catch while both predator and prey are in flight.

They're happy in any forest or woodland environment that supports a diverse community of creatures that will satisfy their appetites and that has old trees with hollows to provide them with secure nesting and roosting sites. These imposing birds have found the perfect habitat not only in the outback but also right on the doorstep of my home.

I've frequently heard their distinctive nocturnal *woof, woof* calls in the forests that surround and merge into my extensive garden and one summer's day, as I woke well before dawn had shrugged off the doona of night, I heard the repetitive voice of a Barking Owl that appeared to be only a few metres from my bedroom.

I crept outside, still in my nightdress and slippers, as the bird's calls continued. As the first feeble rays of sunlight glinted through the forest canopy I scanned the dark vegetation for any signs of life – and my eyes were ultimately met by a stare from golden eyes. I was speechless with wonder and seemingly welded to the spot by the intensity of the Barking Owl's hypnotic gaze, but when I finally moved my eyes there was another wondrous encounter in store. Nearby sat the young bird's parents, glaring down at me with undisguised distain, for I had unwittingly disrupted their diurnal doze.

"You're always welcome in my garden and I'm so pleased to finally see you face to face," I whispered in reverence as each of the birds continued to transfix me with its mesmerising stare.

For the next two weeks the little family remained in the garden, glowering stoically at me as I went quietly and discreetly about my tasks below them. They remained as lethargic and as silent as a shoal of sulking glove puppets but it was a different matter once night had descended, for they 'barked' for hour after endless hour.

I'd grown accustomed to their monotonous and repetitive calls that were simply a means of alerting others of their species to their presence but one night I was jolted from my sleep by an unfamiliar sound, by a bloodcurdling scream and in a moment of panic I assumed that an axe-wielding murderer was perpetrating some grizzly deed, with his victim's voice of terror shattering the tranquillity of the night. Fortunately my fear was unfounded, for what I had heard was only the alarm call of a Barking Owl that, for obvious reasons, is also referred to as a 'Screaming Woman Owl'.

In some regions the population of these majestic birds has declined in recent years, primarily as a result of land clearing and the destruction of the birds' habitat. Foxes and feral cats that compete for limited sources of food have put populations of Barking Owls under additional stress too but fortunately they're thriving in many areas of the country.

I'm honoured to have encountered these imposing birds in the outback and I'm equally honoured to have them as my neighbours, for as highly efficient predators they are invaluable allies in the ongoing battle to control insect pests that, without their assistance, would threaten the survival of many plants within my sprawling organic garden.

Where you'll find them: Barking Owls can be found in forests and woodlands in eastern, northern, southern and south-western regions of the Australian mainland.

Black Kite
Milvus migrans

With an estimated global population of six million birds spread throughout Europe, Asia, Africa and Australia, the Black Kite is believed to be the world's most abundant raptor. Few would be foolish enough to claim that this bird of prey, with its dark brown plumage and distinctively forked tail, is among the most attractive of birds but this efficient predator always attracts my attention.

Many years ago, standing alone on the outback plains of western New South Wales with my long hair blown into a tangle by an icy winter wind, I imagined, rather naively, that a solitary Black Kite was performing its aerial display in the azure sky for no other purpose than to entertain me and to provide me with an unforgettable moment of pleasure. I'm older and wiser now but whenever I see either a solitary bird or an immense flock of this common species I still stop and stare in wonder and I'm as enthralled by the spectacle as I was when I first witnessed the aerial agility of this elegant creature.

I've been entertained by the antics of Black Kites on countless occasions and have met them in many locations, from the outback to the coast. I've seen huge flocks clustered around a bloodied roadside carcass of a kangaroo, some tucking into the free feast while others, their appetites sated, preen their feathers while perched on the branches of a nearby tree. And I've watched their mates circling overhead, twirling and gliding gracefully through the sky as they impatiently await their turn to indulge in a second course. At times, in a moment of panic, the feeding birds flee when I appear on the scene but as I wait quietly, motionlessly, the lure of the feast draws them back and overrides the initial timidity they had shown and as they gorge themselves they pay little heed to a humble audience of one.

It was at a most unlikely birdwatching spot that I was treated to the most stunning performance by these gregarious predators. I'd arrived at the rubbish dump on the edge of the South Australian outback town of Innamincka merely to dispose of an accumulation of food scraps and other waste but I found myself standing in reverent silence, forgetting the bulging plastic bags in my hands and almost immune to the less than pleasant surroundings, to the acrid smoke of melting plastic, to the subtle sound of glass shattering in the flames of a smouldering fire and to the smell of the putrefying refuse that had attracted these scavenging birds of prey. I was glued to the spot, unable to divert my eyes from the immense cast of birds that tumbled and spiralled down towards the earth before hitching a ride on an unseen thermal that carried them aloft and sent them, with barely a flutter of their wings, twirling around and around again and again, soaring higher and higher into the sky before gliding back down to earth where, with barely a muted twitter or a feeble squawk, each snatched a morsel of food before repeating its immaculately choreographed dance.

Life for Black Kites, which are also known as 'Fork-tailed Kites', was definitely meant to be easy, for in a land routinely ravaged by the brutal hand of drought there's always plenty of food for scavengers that play an important role in cleaning up the landscape. These magnificent birds are also extremely competent hunters and with their prey including reptiles, rodents, small mammals and large insects, there's always food on the table for these far from fastidious raptors.

Where you'll find them: The species' Australian range covers the majority of the mainland and although their varied habitats range from riverbank woodlands to the sprawling plains of the outback, they are absent from the extreme south-western and south-eastern corners of the continent.

Pacific Baza

Aviceda subcristata

It's not hard to comprehend the reason for the alternative common names of the Pacific Baza, for 'Crested Hawk' refers to the distinctive crest on the bird's head and 'Chicken Hawk' is a reference to the fact that this beautiful predator occasionally preys on farmyard poultry.

Pacific Bazas usually hunt their prey among the treetops of the woodland areas that they inhabit and I've often seen them sitting around taking life at a pace rivalling that of a barnacle shuffling from one coastal rock pool to another but in reality these are far from lethargic creatures. They're simply demonstrating their patience as they wait for their prey to wander through their realm and they're quick to react when they spot a potential victim. Small mammals, reptiles, the chicks of other birds and even native fruits form part of their diet but it's invariably crunchy grasshoppers, fluttering stick insects, well-camouflaged preying mantids and succulent frogs that they find almost irresistible. They have the ability to fly in silence, a skill that's exactly what an efficient aerial predator requires and when they're hunting Pacific Bazas glide silently through the trees, with their talons extended and snatch their unsuspecting prey from among the vegetation or from the air before the doomed creature has time to panic.

My first and most memorable encounter with a Pacific Baza was in the rainforest section of my extensive garden. One summer's day, as the temperature soared to a sizzling 40 degrees, I was sitting on a shaded bench watching the antics of the varied birds that had arrived to drink and to bathe in the cool waters of a bird bath. Finches, scrubwrens and honeyeaters had all been coming and going but suddenly, as a dark shadow passed overhead and a Pacific Baza arrived, with its great wings almost brushing my face, they vanished from the scene as quickly as an excess of mayonnaise dribbles from a sandwich.

'Oops!' the shocked expression on the raptor's face seemed to say as it realised that, being only two metres from the bird bath, I was perhaps a little too close for comfort but the necessity to quench its thirst overcame any trepidation of being in such close proximity to a human, or perhaps it was simply aware that I posed no threat to its survival.

"Take your time mate. The other birds have already had their turn so there's no hurry for you to leave," I whispered as the glamorous raptor, clearly stressed by the intense heat, settled down in the bird bath with its face revealing its pleasure at the relief that the water offered.

Among the dense foliage of nearby shrubs a host of small birds were keeping a low profile. Many species are far from impressed when a Pacific Baza invades their territory and some, like a mob of vigilantes, persistently harass these large raptors and do their best to persuade them to move elsewhere. Pacific Bazas are rarely intimidated and stoically ignore the aggressive antics of the neighbourhood watch brigade that, on this occasion, were feeling as debilitated by the heat as the baza itself. At that moment, among the garden's avian community, there was a harmonious attitude of live and let live with not an angry or irate chirp heard or uttered as the Pacific Baza relaxed while other birds waited patiently for an opportunity to return to the water.

Pacific Bazas have adopted my garden as part of their territory and their shrill, repetitious and monotonous calls alert me to the fact that they've made their seasonal return once again. Each year they raise their young in nests that I've yet to discover, for they're well hidden somewhere among the foliage of the tallest of the forest's trees and the first time I'm aware that these highly distinctive raptors have been raising a family right on my doorstep is when I hear a young bird, one that's finally left the security of the nest, pleading for food. As I watch a parent present its offspring with a tasty morsel of food I'm proud to have created an environment that these beautiful birds enthusiastically call their home.

Where you'll find them:
Pacific Bazas inhabit tropical and subtropical forests and woodlands, as well as agricultural areas, in northern and eastern Australia, and are rarely spotted south of Sydney.

Wedge-tailed Eagle

Aquila audax

With a wing span of up to 2.3 metres, the Wedge-tailed Eagle is Australia's largest bird of prey. It satisfies its huge appetite by capturing small kangaroos and wallabies, in addition to possums, bandicoots, birds, reptiles, rodents and occasionally feral cats. In areas infested with large populations of rabbits these great raptors are as happy as a knot of frogs at an annual convention of geriatric grasshoppers, for rabbits are their favourite food and in areas plagued by large populations of rabbits these feral pests account for some 70 per cent of the diet of eagles.

My encounters with Wedge-tailed Eagles have been many and varied. I've watched these majestic birds riding the thermals that allow them to soar through the skies with effortless ease for hours on end and, aided by the invisible hands of breezes, they can reach an altitude of 1,800 metres or more above the earth for the best bird's eye view imaginable. I've seen large flocks feasting on carrion too, for despite being the tough guys of the avian community Wedge-tailed Eagles, in common with many other birds of prey, routinely take the easy option and feast on whatever death has brought to their table.

I cringed a little at the gruesome scene as, one winter's day, I crept stealthily towards the bloodied and disembowelled corpse of a Red Kangaroo that had met its end on the barren plains of outback New South Wales. I certainly wasn't the first to discover the carcass however, for a convocation of more than 20 eagles had already arrived to enjoy the banquet.

The etiquette at Mother Nature's table deems that the largest of creatures are at the top of the pecking order and with Wedge-tailed Eagles never slow to remind smaller carnivores of their place in the hierarchy, crows and Black Kites obediently moved away to allow the eagles to dine. Even within the community of eagles a strict pecking order is invariably enforced, with the most senior birds feeding while others waited patiently for their turn or squabbled among themselves to be next in line to gorge themselves at the feast. Some reluctantly abandoned their meal and fled to the skies as, step by meticulously slow step, I moved silently towards the corpse and eventually, while his mates circled overhead, only one bird remained, his dark, almost black plumage indicating his seniority. "I'm sorry to disturb you," I said with sincerity, "but please don't abandon your meal on my account, for I'll be on my way in little more time than it takes for a mischief of mice to

fight their way out of a wet paper bag." And the great eagle, with blood and gore dripping from its hooked bill, glanced momentarily in my direction and returned its attentions to the carcass as though I was of no more interest than a solitary ant.

The plumage of Wedge-tailed Eagles changes over time with young birds having golden-brown plumage while adults wear predominantly dark brown or almost black feathers and it was a young bird that I had the pleasure of meeting at a remote Aboriginal community in the Northern Territory. It was perched on a high fence at the edge of the township and its expression as I walked by on my way to my parked vehicle was easy to read. "If you're wondering whether I'm friend or foe then I can tell you right now that I mean you no harm," I said as the majestic bird stared down in my direction. It appeared less concerned by my presence than by that of a mangy dog that was dozing on the dusty ground beneath its feet but even when the dog stood up, stretched, yawned and wandered off almost in a daze, the great bird, intently watching the slow-motion action, appeared unconcerned and remained on its perch where it demonstrated the lethargy of a moulting tiger in a taxidermist's workshop.

In the forested ranges near the sleepy rural settlement of Kalpowar that lies to the north-west of the Queensland city of Bundaberg it was I who was feeling rather lethargic as I headed home after a long and exhausting journey. As the day neared its conclusion, and too tired to drive any further, I settled down on a rocky hillside to serenade the setting sun with my battered guitar and Mother Nature unexpectedly summoned up one of her most skilful aerial performers. In the valley far below me, riding the thermals in a dance that seemed to be synchronised with a poorly played melody, a Wedge-tailed Eagle pirouetted across nature's woodland stage in a mesmerizing and elegant dance that continued until the curtain of night fell and the imposing bird vanished from sight. "An encore please," I shouted with no one to hear me but the eagle had taken its final bow, leaving me with another indelible memory of the beauty of the natural world.

Wedge-tailed Eagles thrive in a wide range of habitats and although I had always assumed that my garden would not be among them, I was abruptly forced to reassess that idea. I'm not the world's greatest wimp but I have to admit that I almost needed a change of underwear when, while watering some shrubs at the edge of a forested section of my sprawling garden, an eagle landed literally at my feet. The breeze from its immense wings ruffled my hair and for a moment time stood still as the great bird and I exchanged stares of shock and awe. The raptor must have been stunned to realise that, while

intent on catching whatever its prey might have been, it had failed to see me and I had been so engrossed in my work that I had failed to notice the majestic bird that had been either perched or flying right above my head. With slow, strained beating of its immense wings it made its laboured retreat and vanished above the tallest of trees leaving me once again speechless with wonder at such an unpredictable encounter.

Since the arrival of Europeans, life has rarely been easy for these great birds of prey. The incessant destruction of forests and woodlands has dramatically reduced the number of potential nesting sites that are available for eagles, many birds have been shot by farmers who regard them as a threat to their livestock and eagles often die after consuming poisoned baits that have been widely distributed across inland areas to control the populations of feral dogs and pigs. The Tasmanian Wedge-tailed Eagle, *Aquila audax fleayi*, with less than 200 pairs surviving in the wild, is listed as endangered but the good news is that, in mainland Australia, these awe-inspiring birds are thriving, and I'm impatiently looking forward to my next enthralling encounter.

Where you'll find them: Wedge-tailed Eagles can be found in Tasmania and throughout mainland Australia with their favoured habitats being woodlands, forested areas and open country.

Whistling Kite

Haliastur sphenurus

With its relatively drab brown plumage the Whistling Kite is perfectly camouflaged in its natural habitat and its distinctive piercing voice is frequently the first clue that this attractive raptor is in the vicinity. I've seen these graceful birds on many occasions but my most memorable encounter was when I was camping beside the Paroo River that trickles past the sleepy New South Wales outback town of Wanaaring.

With a population of merely 80 people Wanaaring is never a hive of activity and the riverside environment, where the bushland is dominated by gnarled eucalyptus trees, is invariably as quiet as a hamburger stall at a dietician's conference. Within minutes of setting up my tent I was in birdwatching mode and with my chair on the riverbank, a cup of coffee in one hand and my camera in the other the dark shadows of the riverbank trees were the only camouflage I needed. I sat silently, motionlessly, barely bothering to glance around, for I knew that the river and the lure of fish would eventually attract the attention of avian predators.

The Whistling Kite whistles when it's in flight and it whistles while it's patiently waiting for its prey to come into view. As its call reverberated across the landscape I knew that my own patience would soon be rewarded by an encounter with this skilful hunter. My excitement was short-lived however, for the kite's voice was obliterated by the angry howl of an approaching storm and as a curtain of black clouds turned day into night and a clap of thunder applauded Mother Nature's intensifying tantrum the bird fell silent. I hastily made my exit too, leaving the next unpredictable act of the performance to the gods of weather that created some wild entertainment that

was dominated by a dazzling light show and horrendous winds that threatened the destruction of both the vegetation and my campsite.

I hoped that the Whistling Kite and other wild creatures had found a sheltered retreat but less than an hour after the angry storm had begun it dissipated and as the sun cautiously peered from behind the retreating clouds the kite began to whistle its monotonous tune once again. "That's not much of a melody mate," I said to the unseen raptor as I glanced around to see where it might be hiding – and I spotted it on a branch overhanging the Paroo River's murky waters. It seemed as though I was invisible, for the bird, with intermittent bouts of whistling, ignored my presence and made repetitive forays to the water, grasped at prey that only it could see and returned to its perch empty handed. As the storm began to rumble in the distance and threatened to return the bird dived down to the water once again and, with a glint of satisfaction in its golden eyes, it snatched a silver fish from the coffee-coloured water.

Whistling Kites enjoy a varied diet, with their prey, in addition to fish and yabbies, including rabbits, reptiles, the chicks of other birds, small mammals and grasshoppers and, when live prey is scarce, they'll go slumming and dine on carrion and thus ensure that they never feel the pangs of hunger.

I'm not one to appreciate the thought of hunger either, so whenever I'm preparing to go camping in the bush I load my campervan up with enough food to feed an invading army – or at least a couple of starving swaggies. In the early days of spring, when I was camping on the wooded banks of Lake Nuga Nuga, in western Queensland's Arcadia Valley, I'd planned to be up early and enjoy a hearty breakfast while I watched the sun rise over the vast shallow lake but I needed no alarm clock to jolt me awake and nag me to crawl out of bed in the darkness. Mother Nature had kindly commandeered one of her little helpers and with a Whistling Kite awake, in action and whistling incessantly well before dawn, sleeping in was definitely not an option.

I hastily kicked Plan B into action, squirmed out of my sleeping bag, tossed on whatever clothes were closest and grabbed a slice of stale bread that would have to suffice as breakfast. I glimpsed momentarily at the shadowy landscape as the lake at its heart was slowly transformed from black to gold and scurried through the trees in pursuit of my unseen prey. I knew exactly where to go and there was no time to waste, for the female Whistling Kite, sitting in her nest in a tall tree at the water's edge, was noisily demanding breakfast and her mate was obligingly searching for whatever he could catch to satisfy her.

He dived into the woodlands to snatch an unsuspecting victim from among the dense foliage of the trees and flew towards the nest to present his offering, but for a while he ignored his mate's mournful calls. The invisible hands of a breeze lifted him high into the clear blue sky, sending him circling dizzyingly round and round and round before a sudden gust of wind hurled him across the sky at lightning speed before allowing him to resume his more leisurely ride on the gently

whirling currents of air. The pleasure of flight seemed to have temporarily outweighed the call of duty – until his mate began to whistle insistently once again. "It's time to stop indulging in fun and get down to the business of feeding your missus," I scolded the bird as it zoomed overhead and he dutifully did as he was told.

These are birds that share my preference for a life of either solitude or with no one other than a life-long mate for company and, like me, they grudgingly come together with others of their kind only when there's an abundance of free food on offer. Every encounter with a Whistling Kite, whether it's been with a flock of these stunningly beautiful raptors or with merely a single bird, has been seared into my memory as a delightful and entertaining experience and I'm itching to get out and about again to satisfy what I have to admit is an addiction to watching these enthralling birds of prey.

Where you'll find them: Whistling Kites can be found throughout the Australian mainland and on rare occasions in Tasmania. Their favoured habitats include both open country and lightly wooded areas that are in close proximity to rivers, wetlands, or other substantial sources of water.

Brown Falcon
Falco berigora

One of Australia's most widespread raptors, the Brown Falcon appreciates its own company more than that of others of its species. It accepts the company of a mate in the breeding season but at other times of the year it's content to live a solitary existence in its extensive range that stretches from coastal regions to the arid outback and all it demands to encourage it to stay is something on which it can perch to obtain an unobstructed view of the landscape and of any prospective prey.

Humans have lent these attractive birds a helping hand with the installation of power poles and, particularly in the absence of trees, these are the Brown Falcons' favoured perches. When they're not sitting quietly, watching and waiting for an unsuspecting victim, a rodent, a small reptile, or an insect to wander into view, these highly efficient predators hover in the air or glide silently across the landscape. I've envied their aerial skills as I've watched them, aided by the most gentle of breezes and without the slightest flutter of their wings, glide effortlessly over sugar cane plantations and newly ploughed farmlands in eastern Queensland and occasionally, when my patience has almost rivalled that of the Brown Falcon itself, I've watched a bird dive to the ground and, in little more than the blink of an eye, return to its perch with its doomed prey held tightly in its talons.

I never become bored with the sight of this species for it's certainly not a case of seen one Brown Falcon, seen them all. These attractive raptors may all be dressed in plumage that's primarily brown but the hue of their attire can vary dramatically, with birds that live in northern tropical areas generally being dark brown, while those in inland regions are a lighter colour, with some, like the glamorous bird that I encountered on a journey through south-western Queensland, wearing vivid chestnut feathers.

As my campervan rattled along a remote and dusty road I spotted a bird perched on the branch of a solitary dead tree that rose from the vast and desolate outback plains. Despite the fact that I stopped my vehicle while the bird was little more than a speck in the distance, it flew off at great speed the moment I stepped out onto terra firma and it quickly became little more than a blur against the azure sky as it hovered among fragments of lacy clouds.

The landscape had been ravaged by the heavy hand of drought and not even a single blade of dead grass rose from the barren red soil that stretched to every distant horizon. I pride myself on

having patience that, at times, rivals that of a ragged scarecrow waiting for a new suit and I took out my camping chair and settled down for what I was sure would be an interminable wait. I was confident that, unless the bird disappeared beyond the horizon, it would eventually have to return to the only dead tree within sight and when my assumption ultimately proved to be correct I struggled to resist the urge to jump up and down with excitement and to shout "Yippee!" as my long wait came to an end with the cautious arrival of the beautiful Brown Falcon.

I remained silent and motionless as the bird fluttered down onto its perch but I couldn't resist an 'I told you so' moment. "I knew you'd be back mate," I whispered as I grinned from ear to ear with satisfaction. "There's nowhere else to go, so you'll just have to ignore me and get on with life as though I wasn't here."

It glared in my direction with a supercilious stare, alternately fixing its eyes on me then glancing momentarily back at the ground, for although the landscape appeared devoid of life, the Brown Falcon, with its astounding eyesight, would detect any hint of a mobile meal.

Brown Falcons are certainly not fastidious when it comes to their diet, with any creature that they can grasp with their talons being on the menu and that means that small mammals and birds, reptiles, insects and rodents are routinely under threat from this elegant predator. In areas with large populations of rabbits this magnificent hunter plays an important role by feasting on these feral animals that, as far as falcons are concerned, are the best bush tucker available.

The Brown Falcon, like all raptors, knows the value of patience and the bird I was watching, although it appeared to be taking life at a leisurely pace, was alert to every fragment of activity within its territory. Its prey had few places to hide and those that might dare to peer out from a subterranean retreat or from behind a stone would discover that death comes at a speed rivalling that of a coven of witches fleeing the wrath of the inquisition.

When it spots its prey, the Brown Falcon swoops down and grabs its victim, putting it out of its misery with one bite with its relatively small yet powerful bill. "It's time for me to head on my way and leave you in peace – and good hunting my friend," I said to the silently perched bird and it acknowledged my voice with a sudden turn of its head and a stern expression that could only have been interpreted as an indication that it was pleased to finally see the back of me.

Where you'll find them: There are few regions in Australia where Brown Falcons cannot be seen at one time or another during the year in their diverse range of habitats that includes open grasslands, outback plains and agricultural areas.

Australian Hobby

Falco longipennis

Spring was the perfect time to spend a few days camping beside the tranquil waters of Lake Nuga Nuga in Central Queensland. It was huge flocks of waterbirds – of Magpie Geese, Black-winged Stilts and Australian Ibises – that were the focus of my attention. Unfortunately my delight at seeing so many glorious birds was countered by despair at the carnage wrought by predatory feral cats. With mauled carcasses of birds strewn along the lake's bank it was obvious that these far from cute and furry moggies had not only eaten their fill of the abundant prey on offer but had also killed birds simply for the thrill of the hunt.

As dusk descended over the landscape I feared for the lives of more birds and was feeling more than a tad depressed by the visual reminders of the threat that the ferocious cats posed to wildlife. I drowned my despair with a cuppa and allowed the tranquil beauty of the landscape to obliterate my sad thoughts until the silence was fractured by an unfamiliar shrill chattering only a short distance away. It reminded me that there was an abundance of life as well as death in this isolated and magical place and I wandered through the woodlands that hem the lake to discover the owner of that curious voice.

It took only a few minutes to spot an Australian Hobby, a raptor that's commonly known as a Little Falcon and that is the smallest of the six species of falcons that call Australia home. It had no qualms about revealing its presence for, perched at the top of a tall dead tree, it was well beyond the reach of the audacious cats that were out and about hunting even during daylight hours. "Who's the king of the castle? You can't catch me," it seemed to be saying as it snubbed its avian nose at the moggies that would be on the prowl somewhere far below.

Australian Hobbies usually hunt at dusk and I watched as the bird launched itself from its perch and, for a few moments, flew low to the ground in search of any unsuspecting prey. With the cupboard bare, it rose skywards to glide stealthily across the treetops where it might be able to catch a small bird that it would skilfully grab while both predator and prey were in flight and, if luck was on its side, the hobby might even capture a bat that would also be out and about as night approached.

The following day I was up early and on the hunt for another glimpse of the hobby. I found it on what appeared to be its favourite treetop perch. From there it had a perfect view of the

landscape and could spot even the smallest of creatures, such as a beetle, a grasshopper, or a cicada, that might walk or flutter into its line of sight while unaware that its fate was to become part of a hungry predator's breakfast menu. The hobby spent endless hours standing motionlessly on its perch, seemingly as lethargic as a moss-covered boulder but all the time it was simply watching and waiting, waiting, waiting for some action – just as I was.

"Patience is definitely a virtue in your case mate but I'm sure you'll eventually be rewarded," I said optimistically as the bird glanced my way with a stern expression that indicated its disapproval of my presence. Taking the hint that I was far from welcome, I made myself scarce and settled down on a log where I was as well camouflaged among the woodland vegetation as a single grain of sand on a beach, but would my patience rival that of the hobby? Probably not, for this is a bird that exhibits the patience of a mummified Egyptian pharaoh waiting for a chariot to transport him to the afterlife.

"Do you want a cuppa? I've just put the kettle on," my other half whispered as he suddenly appeared in the shadows of the forest. Those simple words and the rumbling pangs of hunger were all it took to shatter my patience but the Australian Hobby has no one at its beck and call when hunger becomes intolerable. "I'll be there in less time than it takes for an inebriated penguin to waddle from one iceberg to another," I replied, hoping that, at any moment, I'd be treated to some action and that the bird would obligingly demonstrate its sure-fire method of luring its prey out into the open. "The tucker's on the table so I've got to go," I quietly informed the bird that seemed in no hurry to do anything at all and just as I turned to leave it leapt from its perch, dived into the dense foliage of the nearest trees in the hope of flushing out any tiny creatures that might be hiding there. It emerged with a small lizard wriggling in its talons. As it returned to its favourite perch to savour its meal it turned its head my way once again with a glaring stare that purveyed an unspoken and unmistakable message. "I'll enjoy my feast in private now if you don't mind!"

Where you'll find them: The Australian Hobby is found throughout mainland Australia and in Tasmania. Although open forests and woodlands are its preferred habitat it takes up residence wherever its prey can be found and that includes agricultural regions, wetlands and urban areas that have the appropriate vegetation and ample trees.

PARROTS

Budgerigar
Melopsittacus undulatus

My first encounter with a Budgerigar was when, as a child, I received one as a birthday present. These attractive little parrots, which have come to be known simply as budgies, are the world's most popular pets after dogs and cats, and being amiable creatures that have the ability to mimic human speech it's easy to understand why they've garnered such favour.

My pet bird said little more than 'Good morning, good morning' whatever time of day it happened to be and although some budgies have far greater language skills none have rivalled a little chatterbox named Puck that, according to the *Guinness Book of Records 1995*, had a vocabulary of 1,728 words.

I've often encountered small flocks of these endearing little birds in their natural habitat that is primarily in arid and semi-arid inland regions of Australia. One winter's day, as I wandered through bushland near the remote Queensland town of Boulia, the incessant twittering emanating from the dense foliage of shrubs triggered my curiosity – it was the subtle chorus of a flock of budgies. I waited in impatient silence and they revealed themselves as a swirling cloud of hundreds of birds rushing towards the sky, twirling and cavorting in a chaotic frenzy like autumn leaves tossed into the air by the angry hand of the wind. They vanished from sight before I could fully appreciate their undeniable beauty.

Many of the budgies that have been bred in captivity are dressed in an incredible range of colours, including yellow, white, blue and mauve but every one of the estimated 5 million birds that thrive in the wild looks just as glamorous as its companions despite the fact that all wear an identical green uniform and have a bright yellow face.

Aboriginal people called these charismatic little parrots 'betchegaras', a word meaning something that's good to eat and while it was budgies that were once on the menu of indigenous Australians, the birds themselves know a tasty treat when they find it. Their diet includes the seeds of native grasses and cereal crops together with the succulent leaves and small fruits of herbaceous plants such as saltbush that thrives in vast areas of the outback. Like most other living creatures, they also require water for their survival.

Alerted to the fact that budgies were in the area and determined to get a more intimate look at these charming little characters, I set up camp beside an isolated waterhole and summoned up a hefty serving of patience. With the region being in the grip of a severe drought I was confident that budgies would eventually be drawn to the waterhole that I'd discovered for they never travel far from water. All I had to do was wait.

The best time to see budgies is at dawn or dusk and the next day, well before the sun had made its debut, I settled down, not too comfortably, on the red soil beside the water, confident that, at first light, the birds would arrive to quench their thirst.

A mob of scrawny cattle plodded past in the darkness, squelched through the muddy edges of the waterhole and quietly drank for what seemed to be an interminable time. "Come back later! Please!" I whispered as the first golden rays of the rising sun speared through the surrounding trees. "I'm waiting for some important visitors and they might not appreciate your company."

The cattle obligingly dawdled on their way along a well-worn track and within a nanosecond of their departure, right on cue, a flock of budgies fluttered down to the water's edge.

As some quietly sipped at the murky soup others arrived, with the fluttering performance of the ever-increasing flock punctuated by bouts of argy bargy and incessant twittering and with birds continually coming and going in a blur of vivid green and yellow.

"Who's a pretty boy then?" I whispered as I sat mesmerised by their antics. "Millions of your relatives might be content to live in captivity but long may budgies remain as free as the wind."

Where you'll find them: Budgerigars inhabit woodlands and grasslands in semi-arid and arid inland areas of Australia and although they can be found in many regions of the continent, the far south-west, the northern part of the Northern Territory and the continent's eastern coast are not on their travel itinerary.

Bourke's Parrot

Neopsephotus bourkii

The bone-shaking ride along the dusty and corrugated outback road heading to the Queensland town of Eromanga was almost rough enough to jolt a flock of fossilised dodos back into the land of the living and as every bone in my body rattled and my teeth chattered to the rhythm of the incessant vibrations I was desperate for any excuse to get my feet back onto terra firma. "Stop! Stop! Stop!" I suddenly shouted, hoping that my other half would hear my voice above the mournful growling of our ageing Land Rover. Slamming on the brakes with the panicked expectation that a collision with a kangaroo or other wild creature was imminent, my best mate reined our trusty steed to a halt in a cloud of red dust.

   "It's the perfect spot for a mid-morning cuppa," I replied when, with a hint of displeasure,

he queried my reason for insisting that we should stop right there in the middle of nowhere. I have to admit that I've perfected the art of telling a fib or two, but the smile that crept across my face revealed a hint of my duplicity, for coffee was definitely not my prime concern at that moment. It was a small pool of sapphire blue water among the sparse shrubs that were daubed across the arid landscape that had caught my attention, for in that time of drought any water would be irresistible to birds.

   As my husband obligingly boiled the kettle I positioned my camping chair beside a contorted spiny shrub on the bank of the waterhole and settled down for what I assumed would be an interminable wait, but some quiet avian

activities began before my personal slave had even had time to deliver the coffee and a snack.

Many birds and other wild creatures of the outback routinely drink at dawn or dusk but on that cool winter's morning a pair of Bourke's Parrots made an impromptu appearance and obviously had no concerns about not complying with human expectations.

Unlike most other Australian parrots these relatively small birds are dressed in exceptionally drab attire with the only hint of bling that the male displays being a touch of pale pink and blue among his predominately grey feathers, while the female wears even less impressive plumage. It's the Bourke's Parrots' efficient camouflage and their shy, even reclusive attitude that continually keeps them out of the limelight but they generally appear to have no more complaints about being ignored than a wind-battered scarecrow might have when a family of mice take up residence in its straw-filled trousers. In fact these introverted little birds seem perfectly content to be ignored by everyone and to share the company of only a lifelong mate or a small family group.

They fluttered down to the edge of the waterhole without a single chirp or twitter heralding their arrival and the male, having been alerted to my presence by the chink of a teaspoon as I stirred my coffee, focused his eyes in my direction with a piercing stare that could have stopped the four horsemen of the apocalypse in their galloping tracks. "Don't worry luv, that human will be no more aware of our presence than a dingo would be of a solitary flea meandering through its mangy fur," his quiet yet confident voice and gaze of disdain seemed to imply as he stared alternately at me and at his mate who appeared reluctant to dawdle down to the water. "You definitely got that assumption wrong," I whispered in reply. "You might be well camouflaged among the foliage of mulga trees but here, on this red soil, you're almost as conspicuous as a pair of hippos cavorting across the manicured lawns at a regal garden party."

The timid little parrots remained alert, their eyes continually flicking around to ensure that if any danger came their way they could quickly make their escape to the sky. When a flock of Zebra Finches arrived on the scene, landing beside the water like autumn leaves tossed to the ground by the tantrums of a gale, the Bourke's Parrots made a hasty retreat and vanished from sight. More finches arrived, Galahs and Little Corellas dropped by too. Lunch, courtesy of my well-trained personal waiter, came and went and the avian entertainment continued throughout the day. The Bourke's Parrots, invariably intimidated by a crowd yet never daring to stray too far from water, watched the world around them from the safety of their perch on a dead tree. At mid-afternoon, with a visual inspection confirming that other birds were no longer in the vicinity, they gracefully fluttered down to the ground to continue their quiet way of life and to feed on the seeds of grasses and herbaceous plants.

As the day irrevocably crept to its conclusion I hoped that Budgerigars would make an evening visit to quench their thirst before the curtain of night was draped over another memorable day of birdwatching. As a brief reprieve from a rough journey evolved to become an extended stopover I snuggled down into my sleeping bag and dreamt that, when a new day dawned, the Bourke's Parrots would greet me with a quiet encore performance.

Where you'll find them: These parrots inhabit arid and semi-arid regions with Acacia, Cypress Pine and Eucalypt woodlands from north-western New South Wales and south-western Queensland to the mid-coast of Western Australia. They are also found in an area that stretches from the southern section of the Northern Territory as far south as the South Australian coastal city of Port Augusta.

Eastern Bluebonnet

Northiella haematogaster

With many roads closed due to unseasonal flooding my journey through outback New South Wales had been curtailed and I'd been forced to spend a night at a caravan park on the outskirts of the town of Bourke. It's always easy to spot flocks of Red-tailed Black-Cockatoos, Little Corellas, Sulphur-crested Cockatoos and Galahs here but on this visit I met some less familiar members of the region's avian community.

It's the early bird that gets the worm, so the old saying goes, and it's the early photographer who gets the best photographic opportunities, particularly when wildlife are the prey. On this occasion getting up at the crack of dawn, despite the cold and damp weather that tempted me to stay in my sleeping bag a little longer than usual, certainly paid off.

My plan had been to have a leisurely day and, after breakfast and more cups of coffee than would be good for me, to dawdle down to the nearby Darling River to look for waterbirds and birds of prey that frequent the area. Before I'd gone more than a few metres from my tent Plan A had been abolished and I certainly wasn't complaining, for my simplistic plan was dashed by the most pleasant of surprises. A small group of Eastern Bluebonnets was feeding on the seed heads of grasses and seemed unaware of or merely unintimidated by my presence and I watched them preening and chattering quietly to one another. "We're being watched," one seemed to mutter as it kept one eye on me while continuing to communicate with its mates. "So smile for the camera!" and every bird turned its head in my direction and politely obliged.

Suddenly my other half poked his head out of our campervan and loudly announced that breakfast was ready. "I'll be there in a minute," I replied with a whispered message that he might not have heard but that was accompanied by subtle hand signals that I hoped he'd interpret accurately, signals that said, "There are some birds here that are itching to be photographed," and that meant, if past experiences were anything to go by, that I'd be away for much more than a minute or two. In fact I could almost guarantee that, unless the birds vanished as quickly as a politician's election eve promise, the breakfast would be as cold as a glove puppet in an Arctic blizzard long before I returned to the campervan.

The bluebonnets continued to rummage among the dry grasses that littered the drought-stricken landscape in search of nutrient-rich seeds and insects, for here there were none of the

fruits and flowers that are a welcome delicacy for these endearing little parrots. They usually forage in pairs or in small groups and generously share their territory with larger birds such as Australian Ringnecks and Mulga Parrots, but on this occasion it was Red-winged Parrots that ruled the roost and the bluebonnets appeared less than impressed with the energetic antics of their neighbours that bathed in a muddy puddle. The vigorous flapping of wings, dirty water spraying into the air and onto the blue faces of the little parrots that had come too close for comfort and hierarchical disputes over access to the tiny pool of water became too much commotion for the bluebonnets to tolerate and they made a quiet retreat to the adjacent trees where they sat in the warming sunlight and obligingly posed, once again, for a photo shoot.

Where you'll find them: Bluebonnets are found in many arid and semi-arid inland areas of mainland Australia, from southern Queensland through to New South Wales and from north-western Victoria to south-western Western Australia, where they inhabit plains with low vegetation, open woodlands and grasslands.

Eastern Rosella

Platycercus eximius

Eastern Rosellas can justifiably boast that they're the gaudiest of Australian birds and it was an image on a bottle of tomato sauce that first introduced me to this beautiful parrot that, for many years, was the highly recognisable trademark of the Rosella Preserving and Manufacturing Company. I've seen these glorious birds, in the flesh and feathers, on numerous occasions, primarily in woodlands and urban parklands in southern regions of the continent.

Parrots of any species were thin on the ground when, on a bitterly cold mid-winter's day, I set up camp among the forests that line the shores of Lake Glenbawn, near the New South Wales town of Scone. During my rambling walks I'd spotted many species of aquatic birds drifting on the lake's wind-rippled waters and had spied on others that had made themselves at home in the woodlands that clamber over the hills that embrace the lake. I'd seen them all, or at least a large proportion of them, or so I erroneously assumed and when it was time to leave I packed up my campsite almost as quickly as Peter Piper might pick a peck of pickled peppers and was impatient to head on my way to another spectacular birdwatching destination.

"I'll just have one more quick look around before we go," I said to my ever-patient husband as I set off on what was intended to be a five-minute stroll to the water's edge. Pelicans and flocks of Eurasian Coots were bobbing on the water. Australian King-Parrots were feeding on crumbs that they'd discovered beside a deserted picnic table and Superb Fairy-wrens were twittering

and fluttering in their usual hyperactive fashion among the mayhem of tall grasses that bowed obediently to the whims of an intensifying wind. I watched them all for longer than I had intended to do but it was other birds that captured every fragment of my attention as I dawdled quietly along a meandering track.

A group of Eastern Rosellas was bathing in a muddy puddle, with every bird having not just a lick and a promise type of wash but making a concerted effort to saturate every feather. "I'm not sure how clean you'll get in such dirty water," I queried as the birds, seemingly unconcerned about the near-freezing winter temperature, splashed and frolicked, with their vivid red faces dipping bravely beneath the water in contorted poses and their wings flapping energetically to ensure that every fragment of their rainbow-hued plumage was dripping wet. As one or two birds left the group and settled into the dense foliage of a nearby shrub to preen their sodden plumage others descended to perform the vital ritual, some coming back to bathe time and time again until they appeared so sodden with water that flight, to someone of a species that has never mastered that skill, seemed as though it would be a daunting if not impossible feat. Despite my scepticism, every member of the little flock ultimately took to the air, then, with every colourful feather spotlessly clean and perfectly rearranged, they fluttered down to the ground to rummage among the jumbled vegetation for the seeds of grasses, low-growing shrubs and herbaceous native plants that generously offer the birds a free lunch and with insects, together with the flowers, fruit and nectar of trees and shrubs providing dessert, the delightful Eastern Rosellas were as happy as a swarm of cockroaches in a compost bin.

Where you'll find them: South-eastern Australia, from Queensland to Victoria, and also in south-eastern South Australia and Tasmania, where they inhabit open woodlands and grasslands that have adequate trees for roosting and nesting.

Galah

Cacatua roseicapilla

I still vividly recall my first sighting of a Galah, despite the fact that it was a fleeting moment several decades ago. I'd arrived in Australia as a child migrant and only a few days after setting foot on the shores of South Australia I was with my mother on a train chugging towards the city of Adelaide. Beyond the window lay vast treeless plains and I was mesmerised by the unfolding scenery and enthralled when a flock of unfamiliar birds flew past. "Look Mum! Parrots! Parrots!" I shouted in excitement. "They're just Galahs luv," an elderly man sharing our carriage said with disinterest. "Nothin' ta write home about," yet for a child who had recently arrived from Britain the sight of a flock of wild parrots was a dream come true.

Galahs, which are also known as 'Rose-breasted Cockatoos' or 'Roseate Cockatoos', are one of the most common of Australia's 56 species of parrots and over the ensuing years I've encountered them on countless occasions and in a great diversity of habitats.

The word Galah, which is an adaptation of the Aboriginal word 'gilaa', has come to refer to someone who's playing the fool but despite the connotations of their colloquial name I've rarely seen these birds doing anything that resembles stupidity. I've watched them bathing, feeding, drinking, nesting, doing all the sensible things that come naturally to a bird that seldom demonstrates any hint of tomfoolery or frivolous behaviour and I'm still in awe of the beauty of these birds that, to many people, are 'just Galahs'.

Galahs were my most prominent neighbours when, during the heart of

winter, I camped beside the Ross River that mooches through the West Macdonnell Ranges near the central Australian town of Alice Springs. They arrived on my doorstep at dawn and the small flock fluttered silently down from the shading trees to take advantage of the trickling stream's clear water. Then, chattering quietly yet intently to one another as though whispering the secrets of the universe, they meandered through the emerald grasses, feeding on the bounty of seeds. With their focus on a feast they ignored my calculated and hesitant movements and the muted sounds I made as I filled the kettle with water, made myself a cuppa and settled down to my own breakfast under the awning of my campervan from where I could enjoy an unobtrusive glimpse into their lives.

It was more threatening sounds than mine that eventually attracted the Galahs' attention and as the howl of Dingoes echoed among the rocky hills the birds glanced in the direction of the predatory canines, glanced at each other and glanced nervously at me with the unspoken expectation that I might volunteer to be their saviour. "You mob look as happy as an Emu that's realised that its destiny is to become a feather duster," I said as the Galahs became increasingly agitated. "All I can suggest is that you head for the trees before the Dingoes arrive and expect to have Galah on their menu." The birds, perhaps with the same thoughts on their minds, took the hint, fluttered to safety and had soon vanished among the dense foliage of the old and gnarled gum trees that dipped their contorted roots into the river's water.

Galahs, like many other Australian parrots, require trees with substantial hollows that they can use when nesting and on the banks of Cooper Creek, near the South Australian outback settlement of Innamincka, the River Red Gums that line this iconic stream provide an abundance of quality accommodation. Within minutes of my late afternoon arrival at this isolated location Galahs had begun to move into the arboreal apartments that towered above my campsite.

Those that had claimed ownership of a hollow were as content and quiet as ravenous caterpillars in a cabbage patch but for others there were continual disputes regarding ownership with some birds, with stoic determination and incessant screeching, aggressively defending their territory as others attempted to evict them.

I'm well practised in the art of whinging and as vociferous conflicts continued to erupt long after darkness had crept across the landscape I couldn't keep quiet any longer. "It's time you lot made a declaration of peace, at least for tonight," I called to the noisiest of avian agitators but the screeching intensified and as the birds ignored my plea I admitted what I'd known all along, that verbal persuasion would have no impact on their rowdy behaviour and that I'd have as much chance of holding back the ocean's

advancing tide with a few stern words as I would of obtaining a little peace and quiet that night.

The next day tranquillity reigned and I crawled out of my sleeping bag to find the birds peacefully rummaging for food among the tangled vegetation at the creek's edge. It was the seeds of grasses and other low plants that satisfied their appetite here but Galahs, like most Australian parrots, can't resist the lure of cultivated grain crops and huge flocks, disputing the statement that there's no such thing as a free lunch, routinely gorge themselves in farmers' fields.

These are birds that demonstrate great resilience and during a drought in the early 1990s a large flock of Galahs, in search of food and water, moved into the rural town that's on my doorstep and have never left. I see them every day as they feed on the grass of urban parklands and the local golf course, perform acrobatic antics on overhead power cables and flutter through the skies from one shading tree to another, and I'm still excited by a glimpse of these wild parrots that are just Galahs.

Where you'll find them: Galahs can be found throughout Australia, with the exception of the furthest tip of the Cape York Peninsula in Queensland and the south-western corner of Western Australia. They thrive in arid and semi-arid regions and are frequently seen in urban areas but the largest flocks, which may include hundreds of birds, inhabit open woodlands and grasslands where there are scattered trees in which the birds can shelter and roost.

Little Corella
Cacatua sanguinea

Little Corellas elicit either love or hate and occasionally I've exhibited both emotions when I've encountered hordes of these white cockatoos. I've seen them in urban areas and in remote corners of the outback and I've watched, with quiet admiration, as each bird in an immense flock snuggles up to and affectionately preens the feathers of its life-long mate. I've seen them fluttering among the golden blooms of native Silky Oak trees (*Grevillea robusta*) and clambering among clusters of Eucalyptus flowers to silently sip the sweet nectar. I've watched them nibbling on the seeds of grasses, legumes and ripening crops of grain and I can't help but admire these resilient and attractive cockatoos but when the same flock of birds has revealed the flip side of their character I've cursed them and wished that they and I were a million miles apart.

An encounter with a single Little Corella is almost as rare as the chance of spotting an octopus strolling through a rainforest for these are the most gregarious of birds that invariable hang out with a huge gang of their mates and they're never short of something to chirp, squawk or screech about.

On a scorching mid-summer's day that would have made even Beelzebub feel a little hot under the collar I dawdled through the parklands in the Queensland city of Maryborough and loitered beneath the line of shading trees that flank the park's extensive lagoon, where I found myself in quiet company. A large flock of Little Corellas was relaxing among the trees' dense foliage with most doing nothing more energetic than, in a genuine display of affection, preening their mate's plumage with a delicate touch. I admired them for their gentle and caring ways and for their conspicuous passion for their companions but Little Corellas are not always so affable.

In a more remote location, near the South Australian outback town of Innamincka, I watched their frenetic activities as they fluttered among the great River Red Gums that hem the tranquil waters of Cooper Creek and that cast their lofty shadows over my campsite. Each bird and its mate was determined to claim a secluded hollow for their nesting site but with limited accommodation available serious disputes erupted, not only between Little Corellas, for Red-rumped Parrots and Galahs were also searching for somewhere secure to raise a family and the corellas had instigated a no-holds-barred campaign of attack. There were no niceties here, other than between a bird and its mate, for this was outright warfare with a place to nest and the chance to guarantee the survival of the species being the winner's ultimate prize.

Well away from the arboreal battlefield, on a log protruding from the creek's murky waters, other corellas were quietly drinking and bathing, safe here even from the Dingo that silently prowled along the creek's far bank. Suddenly, when it seemed that both the birds and I were as content with that moment of our lives as a swarm of flies in a dustbin, a Whistling Kite, issuing a screech of alarm as a second Dingo strode confidently into view, flew too close for comfort and the corellas, in a moment of panic, fled to the safety of the skies. All I could do was watch the varied actors on nature's stage and hope that the Dingoes would eventually leave to hunt elsewhere.

Little Corellas often hang out together with hundreds of their mates and they're a raucous and argumentative lot, not only when they're squabbling over nesting sites but also when they settle down to roost for the night. On many occasions I've set up camp in a tranquil rural location and, just as I'm admiring a gaudy sunset and appreciating the serenity and solitude of the environment, a pandemonium of corellas has arrived on the scene. Initially I've been pleased to see them but when the argy bargy has begun I've been far from impressed with the rowdy neighbours that have decided to make themselves at home right on my doorstep.

Nightfall has invariably brought a reprieve from vocal mayhem but the chaos has resumed the moment dawn peeps from the darkness and when the Little Corellas have finally decided to search for the first snack of the day their departure has been accompanied by noise that would put a gaggle of screeching banshees to shame as they launch themselves into the air from their lofty perches. Like fragile snowflakes at the mercy of a gale they make their exit in a blizzard of white plumage to gorge themselves on any seeds they can find and their insatiable appetite for crops of grain ensures that Little

Corellas, as far as farmers are concerned, are as welcome as a skunk in a French perfume factory.

When food and water are in short supply in the corellas' natural habitat huge flocks of these rowdy birds take what is the only option in their bid for survival and invade urban areas. Here it's more than their incessant noise that guarantees that they never receive a warm welcome. Thousands of birds defecate on parked vehicles, on pathways and on park benches and the destructive little blighters rip at the leaves of trees to such a degree that some, stripped of every skerrick of foliage, eventually die as a result of the actions of the uninvited vandals.

I admit that I'm not always happy to see large populations of Little Corellas but my complaints are muted by the knowledge that the birds are only doing what comes naturally to them and whenever I mutter a few words of displeasure at their noisy behaviour I'm sure I can hear the boss cocky of the group informing me that "If you don't like it, then it's you who should be leaving, not us."

Where you'll find them: These corellas can be found in the majority of mainland Australia's semi-arid and arid regions and can also be seen in many urban areas.

Major Mitchell's Cockatoo

Lophochroa leadbeateri

The common name of this stunning cockatoo honours Major Thomas Mitchell who, in the 19th century, was the New South Wales Surveyor General and one of the young nation's most daring adventurers. "Few birds more enliven the monotonous hues of the Australian forest than this beautiful species," Mitchell wrote of the bird that would later immortalise his name and, having seen this cockatoo in the wild, I certainly wouldn't disagree with that statement.

Major Mitchell's Cockatoos are usually seen in pairs or small groups but they'll occasionally congregate in flocks of 50 or more if there's permanent water and an abundance of food available.

Whenever I'm in the arid inland regions that Major Mitchell's Cockatoos inhabit I keep my eyes wide open for a conspicuous clue that these birds are in the vicinity and one spring day, when

driving along an outback Queensland road near the less than one horse town of Eromanga, I spotted exactly what I had been looking for. Wild melons. The thought of a banquet of wild melons is as enthralling to me as the idea of spending a long weekend in a leaking submarine, but this is a fruit that is absolutely irresistible to Major Mitchell's Cockatoos.

Being in no hurry to get to my next destination I opted to test my patience and to loiter at the roadside to see if the melons would attract the attention of any birds and I didn't have long to wait, for these cockatoos' reaction to the sight of melons is as predictable as the fate of a chocolate teapot.

A solitary bird fluttered down

to the ground as though I was invisible, which was the concept I was hoping for as I stood motionlessly in the grey shadow of my campervan. With a blur of pink feathers the cockatoo quickly grabbed the small green melon and flew, with its prize grasped firmly in its bill, to the highest branch of a dead tree.

Just as I began to creep slowly towards it a motorist stopped to enquire if my vehicle had a problem and if I needed assistance but he unexpectedly changed his tune from one of a good Samaritan when I told him that I was hoping to capture some photos of the cockatoo that was merely a few metres away. "You're wasting your time," he said with unexpected aggression in his voice. "You'll never get within a mile of a Major Mitchell's Cockatoo."

These lovely birds are, without doubt, notoriously timid but I was confident that any bird that has its claws on a wild melon wouldn't abandon its favourite food too hastily and time and patience proved me right. Ignoring the stranger's pessimistic comments I began to sneak quietly towards the bird that, although it was aware of my approach, had one eye on its prize and one steadfastly on me but it made no attempt to leave. The melon was too delicious to abandon. Then, suddenly, the other driver slammed the door of his vehicle, revved the motor viciously and the bird, discarding its feast, vanished at high speed. "With two more brain cells you could qualify for the position of village idiot mate," I muttered in frustration at the driver as his vehicle's spinning tyres showered me with a cloud of dust and brought my encounter with one of Australia's most beautiful birds to an abrupt conclusion.

During another outback adventure near Rainbow Valley, south of Alice Springs, I encountered

a flock of more than 50 Major Mitchell's Cockatoos. It was once again wild melons that had captured their attention and I'd been able to tiptoe into the shadow of a rocky outcrop from where, unseen, I silently watched the group's feeding frenzy. While some birds gorged themselves on the flesh and seeds of their favourite bush tucker others flew low above the ground, twirling and tumbling in a mesmerising display of aerial agility that exposed the vivid orange plumage beneath their outstretched wings. They seemed as addicted to the pleasures of the banquet as a knot of frogs at an annual convention of geriatric grasshoppers and as the sun stealthily slid towards the distant horizon I left them to enjoy their party and dawdled on my way to my next destination.

Major Mitchell's Cockatoos, in addition to their passion for wild melons, also feed on insects and fruit, together with the seeds of Acacia and Cypress Pine trees, both of which are dominant species in many of the outback regions that these beautiful birds call home. The optimum time to see these glorious creatures is at dawn or dusk when they arrive on the banks of waterholes and streams to quench their thirst. If melons are growing nearby they'll be drawn to them as irresistibly as a redback spider is attracted to the darkest corner of an outback dunny. I hope that I'll be privileged to see these birds on many more occasions.

Where you'll find them: They inhabit open woodlands in arid and semi-arid areas in south-western Queensland, New South Wales, the Northern Territory and Western Australia. Land clearing and the resultant destruction of the habitat of the Major Mitchell's Cockatoo began in the first years after European settlement and by the 1950s the species had disappeared from most of South Australia. Their populations have also declined in western New South Wales and in north-western Victoria where, although still found in the mallee region, this cockatoo is now listed as a threatened species. The good news is that its future is secure in many other areas.

Mulga Parrot

Psephotus varius

As I drove through south-western Queensland I was feeling almost as miserable as an ageing centipede with bunions on its 50 left feet. It was the outback landscape that had triggered my grey mood, for it had been brutally battered by years of drought and every shrub and tree, with its wilting and yellowing foliage, seemed to be hinting that it was almost at death's door. When I reached my ultimate destination the scene was even more depressing.

In the remote Culgoa Floodplain National Park, Nebine Creek is rarely more than a lethargic stream that meanders across the plains. It had been reduced to little more than a series of stagnant pools and clearly if the punishing drought continued every drop of water would soon vanish into oblivion.

I attempted to shrug off negative thoughts of what a future created by global overpopulation and climate change might hold for the outback and for the Earth itself but there was no use denying that things would get far worse if rain remained as rare as the legendary bunyip that makes itself at home in outback swamps and billabongs. Many birds and animals

would inevitably die and vulnerable species might be driven into the abyss of extinction but, being an eternal optimist, I donned my rose-tinted glasses, banished thoughts of the worst-case scenario from my mind and focused only on the surviving, yet less conspicuous aspects of the outback's natural beauty.

It was late afternoon and the sun was in retreat when I set up camp beside the remnants of the creek and although any positive effects of drought are generally elusive, I was confident that the drought would guarantee that Mother Nature, with a cast of diverse characters at her beck and call, would still be able to stage a memorable performance.

I was certain that she would summon up a chorus of birds that would congregate around the muddy pools that offered them their only chance of survival in the harsh environment but as I settled down on a log at the water's edge there was less activity than in a crypt full of Egyptian mummies. For a moment I thought that perhaps the drought had already extinguished every hint of life but as dusk descended over the landscape the first act of the evening's entertainment began. A large mob of Red Kangaroos peered cautiously from the low woodlands and bounded joyfully down to the water's edge where males and females, young and old lined up side by side to drink – but there was not a single bird in sight.

The next day I was out and about before dawn and watched the kangaroos return to the water

as the first glimmer of sunlight peered through the trees, but this time they were accompanied by a motley crew of other outback characters, by Brown Treecreepers, Galahs, Red-rumped Parrots and White-plumed Honeyeaters that were all desperate to quench their thirst.

I was thirsty too but I was reluctant to abandon my waterfront seat and risk missing some unanticipated highlight of the non-stop avian activities. Fortunately my husband, emerging from the campervan rubbing sleep from his eyes, came to the rescue and soon had the kettle boiling and breakfast cooking. The stirring of porridge, the clink of cutlery, the slurping of tea and whispered words passing between myself and my best mate went unheard or were simply ignored by the diverse cast of performers who danced across the muddy pool that was the central feature of nature's outback stage. A kangaroo and her exuberant joey arrived and engaged in a little argy bargy at the water's edge as the mother, with snarling and a swift clip around the ear with a long-clawed paw, roughly instructed her offspring about the etiquette of life. At that first hint of discord a mayhem of squawks and twittering erupted and the warning was passed around, "Let's get out of here before she takes her temper tantrum out on us too!" and every bird made a frantic dash for the safety of the trees.

As the kangaroos finally hopped back to the bushland and tranquillity returned the birds fluttered down to the water, with a group of Mulga Parrots joining the cheerful throng. Male Mulga Parrots are the celebrities of the avian world and these vain and glamorous birds, in their dazzling blue-green turquoise attire, always put on an ostentatious display. As three of the little fellas paraded before me, sauntering backwards and forwards as though wandering along an unseen catwalk and pirouetting slowly and gracefully around to show off every aspect of their glorious attire, I was spellbound by the stars of the moment.

With an arrogant and haughty air they seemed to say "Look at us! Aren't we the most beautiful birds you've ever seen?" And their audience, which included a small group of meek and unassuming females dressed in nothing other than drab grey-brown plumage, could, like me, do nothing other than agree.

With the parade concluded, the Mulga Parrots, which usually live with a mate or in a small family group, turned their attention to food and dawdled along the creek's shaded banks searching among scattered clumps of dry grass and low herbaceous plants for the seeds, flowers and insect larvae that are the main ingredients of their diet. "The tucker must be good," I whispered as the little birds gradually came closer and closer. "Oi! I'm talking to you!" I added with a hint of surprise that none of the little group had acknowledged my presence. "I'm sitting here quietly so that I don't disturb you but a glimpse in my direction every now and then so that I could see your lovely faces would be appreciated." As if it had comprehended every word, a male bird looked up, glaring in my direction – and I'd rather it hadn't, for if I could have accurately read the facial expression and body language of that gaudy little character it would have said, without a doubt, "Just clear off and let us get on with our feast."

Eventually, with their appetites sated, the Mulga Parrots fluttered down to the water, leaning down from partially submerged logs and contorted branches not only to drink but also to admire their reflections in the water's mirror surface. "We really are the most beautiful of outback birds, aren't we?" a male seemed to ask as it momentarily glanced my way. And how could I do anything other than concur?

Where you'll find them: These parrots inhabit semi-arid areas in all mainland states of Australia. They prefer areas with open woodlands that are dominated by Acacias, Eucalypts, Cypress Pines (*Callitris*) or She Oaks (*Casuarina* species) and where there is a ground cover of low shrubs, spinifex grass or samphire. They can be found in south-western Queensland, west of the Great Dividing Range in New South Wales, in the mallee country of north-western Victoria, throughout much of South Australia and in some southern areas of Western Australia.

Red-rumped Parrot

Psephotus haematonotus

These unpretentious little parrots make no great song and dance about their presence and the first time I encountered a pair they were, despite their energetic activities, as quiet as a couple of worms getting a wriggle on across a glacier. They were probably feeling almost as cold too, as on a chilly mid-winter's day they bathed in the shallow waters at the edge of the Darling River that meanders through the New South Wales outback.

Birds had been the last thing on my mind as I stood beside my campsite on the river's wooded bank, for there was wild weather on the way and this corner of the world was about to get a battering. I watched with some concern as black clouds hung like prophets of doom over the woodlands where even the largest of trees bowed to his majesty the wind as, with an angry growling voice, he made his way inexorably across the landscape. The Red-rumped Parrots, the male with his predominantly turquoise-green plumage and vivid red rump and his mate attired in drab grey feathers, seemed unconcerned as the storm continued its approach, but when a violent flash of lightning and accompanying thunder shook the ground beneath my feet they needed no more reason to retreat to a secluded hollow in a riverbank log. "Are you coming inside" the female seemed to say as, with a panicked squawk, she peered out at her mate, "or do you think you're tough enough to survive out there?" And with no additional persuasion required her partner dashed into the couple's waterfront home with a view.

In subsequent years I've seen these charming birds in many outback regions and, unlike larger parrots, they rarely seem to be any more aggressive than a steaming Yorkshire pudding. In the ancient River Red Gums that stand like sentries along the banks of Cooper Creek, near the South Australian outback settlement of Innamincka, Little Corellas and Galahs argued over every hollow that could become a valuable nesting site with each pair berating others with a squawking tongue lashing that was harsh enough to strip the hide from a rampaging rhino, but at the Red-rumped Parrots' residence there was no hint of argy bargy. When other birds approached these courteous little parrots simply poked their heads out of the hole as if to politely say "Sorry! This apartment is already taken," and with the message clearly understood and realising that they were as welcome as butchers at a vegetarians' convention the intruders subserviently fluttered away.

Red-rumped Parrots, like many other Australian parrots, spend their lives with the same mate and, on the rare occasion that one is on its own it appears as miserable as Tweedledum without Tweedledee. They feed primarily on the seeds of grasses but will also snack on the fruits and flowers of some shrubs and trees and are very partial to the leaves and flowers of certain species of thistles. As they forage on the ground or among dense foliage there's barely a murmur from these most demure of parrots.

Where you'll find them: Red-rumped Parrots frequent semi-arid regions of south-eastern Australia, including those in New South Wales and Victoria, with lesser populations also existing in north-eastern South Australia and south-western Queensland. They inhabit lightly wooded grasslands and mallee scrub and make themselves at home in urban parks and gardens within their range.

Red-winged Parrot

Aprosmictus erythropterus

My first encounter with Red-winged Parrots was a tame affair, for although the birds that I saw in a friend's garden near the Queensland town of Mount Perry were wild, they had become accustomed to the ways of the human race and were only there to accept the offer of a free lunch of sunflower seeds. Feeding the birds had long been a daily ritual for my friend and the ravenous hordes arrived on cue at the regular time with every Red-winged Parrot within earshot aware that discovering food in this neck of the woods was as easy as winning a game of tiddlywinks with a geriatric one-eyed teddy bear. All they had to provide in return for an all-you-can-eat buffet was a display of their unrivalled beauty.

When there's an abundance of food and water within their range large flocks of Red-winged

Parrots are a relatively common sight. These colourful birds often spend their days in the company of only their mate or a small group of companions. They forage among grasses and foliage and feed on seeds, flowers, nectar, fruit and even insects, with the seeds of Eucalyptus and Acacia trees and the berries of parasitic Mistletoe being among their favoured foods.

The males of the species, when they're fending for themselves and feeding on open ground, are as conspicuous as a skulk of foxes in a hen house but when they're going about their daily lives in higher vegetation they're extremely well camouflaged and often heard before they're seen, for their presence is betrayed only by an array of sounds that range from quiet twittering and whistling as they communicate with others of their flock, to a piercing screech of alarm at the approach of a predator or a human who has wandered into their territory.

On a winter's day, when a deluge had closed outback roads and forced a change to my travel plans, I sought temporary refuge at a caravan park in the New South Wales town of Bourke. When a new day dawned with the threat of more wet and cold weather I became uncharacteristically irritable and sullen and my other half, being far from impressed with my grey mood, tactfully hinted that, with the rain having eased momentarily, I should go outside and get some fresh air.

I soon found that I wasn't the only one appreciating a few moments of 'dry' weather, for just beyond my doorstep a small group of Red-winged Parrots – mum, dad and a couple of juveniles – were taking advantage of a muddy puddle to drink and bathe. "You're certainly a most glamorous family," I whispered as the male gazed at his reflection in the water while his mate preened herself and the youngsters nibbled at the stems of grasses that were bent to the ground under the weight of raindrops.

"There's a cuppa ready if you're not so grumpy now," my other half called as he stepped outside the campervan and before I could reply the Red-winged Parrots had fled, with only the male still in the vicinity. He'd discovered a wild melon growing nearby and was not about to abandon what is the favoured food of many inland parrots, but as other campers wandered in his direction retreat seemed his only option and, grasping his prize in his bill, he flew to a nearby tree to enjoy a special treat.

Where you'll find them: This parrot's range, which includes arid and semi-arid regions of the continent, extends from northern Australia, throughout Queensland and as far south as north-eastern South Australia, with the birds' varied habitats including riverine forests, acacia scrub and open woodlands.

Superb Parrot

Polytelis swainsonii

When I'm travelling through the bush and midday arrives I rarely visit a café or a pub for a meal – I'd rather settle down with a simple snack in a quiet and shaded environment where there's the chance of spotting some wildlife. The location I discovered on an August day, near the New South Wales rural town of Warren, was simply a wide strip of eucalypt forest that separated the less than busy road from treeless farmlands, but it was quiet, shady and pleasant enough and while I waited for the kettle to boil the water for a cuppa, I wandered off to explore the environment.

An unfamiliar and subtle twittering caught my attention and I slowly, stealthily, quietly moved through the trees in pursuit of whatever bird might be here. My other half, the chief cook and bottle washer on every excursion, called out that lunch was ready but it was not food that would satisfy my appetite at that moment, for I was on the trail of something that, I was confident, was rather special. I was speechless with wonder when I finally spotted my quarry, a parrot that, with its vivid green plumage, yellow face and red streaked throat was stunning enough to justify its name, for the Superb Parrot is indeed superb.

"You might have thought you were being quiet but you weren't quiet enough to prevent me from finding you, so ta very much for allowing me to make your acquaintance," I whispered as the bird stared down from its lofty perch. "Where did you come from?" it seemed to ask as though it had, until that moment, been completely unaware of my presence. "Don't worry mate," I replied to its stare of surprise, "I'll just stand here and be as quiet as a weevil in a sack of rice, so you can get on with whatever you were doing and just ignore me." The bird, still staring intently with its dark and glinting eyes, seemed to accept that assurance and resumed pecking at the branch, picking off tiny insects, before fluttering onto the ground to feed on the seeds of dying grasses that a winter's frost had turned to gold.

The twittering that had initially alerted me to the bird's presence resumed unexpectedly and a small group arrived, seemingly as curious to see me as I was to see them. "Have you seen one of these creatures before?" they seemed to be enquiring of each other with their soft melodic voices, so I stood silently, motionlessly and allowed them to gradually come closer to see the strange human animal that had dropped by to visit them.

Superb Parrots are usually seen in small family groups and there are believed to be less than 5,000 breeding pairs left in the wild. Their diet consists of the seeds of grasses and herbaceous plants as well as berries, flowers, nectar and insects and with abundant grain crops in the areas that they inhabit they never go hungry. It's wide scale land clearing that poses the greatest threat to their survival. In some areas the old trees that provide the hollows they need for nesting have become as rare as a wink from a whistling wombat, so life is far from easy for these magnificent birds.

Where you'll find them: Superb Parrots inhabit woodlands that are close to waterways. Listed as a vulnerable species they are found only in south-eastern Australia, primarily in the Riverina area of New South Wales and Victoria. They travel extensively within their range, with some birds migrating and spending the coldest winter months in central and northern New South Wales, where they take up residence close to the Namoi and Gwydir Rivers.

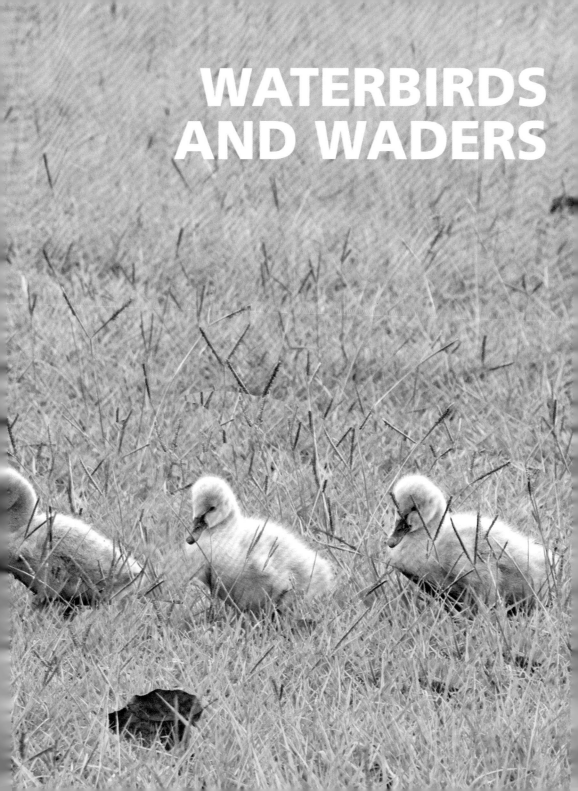

WATERBIRDS AND WADERS

Black Swan

Cygnus atratus

When, as a migrant child, I first saw a Black Swan on the banks of the Torrens River that dawdles through the heart of the city of Adelaide I assumed it was an aberration, some weird mutation, for all I'd ever known was the gleaming white Mute Swan of Britain. My amazement mirrored that of earlier European visitors to Australia who, like me, assumed that all swans were white, but that concept was turned on its head in 1636 when a sailor on board the Dutch ship *Banda* sighted a Black Swan near an island off the south-western coast of Australia.

The Black Swan is a bird that Australians now look upon with pride and this majestic creature has been elevated to a position of prominence as the state emblem of Western Australia and also features on that state's flag.

Like many waterbirds, Black Swans have adopted urban parks that have large bodies of water as their habitat and although I've watched them pleading for food from humans who are all too willing to oblige by providing the birds with bread and other junk food, I prefer to see swans in a more natural environment.

The forested landscape surrounding the Kolan River, north of the Queensland city of Bundaberg, is as welcoming to birds as an Irish pub would be to a family of leprechauns. As I paddled my kayak slowly along the river I saw a cygnet, a young swan in its overcoat of fluffy grey plumage, drifting aimlessly on the calm water. I cautiously edged closer, expecting it to vanish from the scene, but it merely stared in my direction with a dazed expression that I interpreted as an indication that it was perhaps injured or unwell. I drifted alongside the cygnet and, leaning over the side of the kayak, I gently picked it up. Although it was far heavier and more cumbersome than the bundle of feathers that I had assumed it would be, I placed it on my lap and paddled to the bank where I could examine it. "Let's have a good look at you mate," I whispered with compassion. "If you've been injured and need some help, getting you to a vet could be a task that's about as easy as sifting eels through a tea strainer but I'll see what I can do."

I carefully unloaded my sedentary and obliging passenger and sat it on the ground. While I examined each wing and each webbed foot it gave barely a fidget of concern, but then suddenly, in response to a honk from an adult somewhere upstream, it stood up, raced towards the river with its wings flapping wildly and paddled as fast as its little legs and feet could take it.

"Are you a malingerer or were you simply looking for a new, exciting and different experience, a touch of adventure to brag about to your mates?" I asked and as I stood, bewildered, on the riverbank, the young bird vanished among the vegetation and I wondered, for a fleeting moment, if I had simply imagined its existence and its amazing behaviour.

Later that day, I discovered a swan's nest concealed among the grasses and reeds at the river's edge. Actually I tell a lie, for I only realised that the nest was there when a swan, raised up to its full height and with its wings outstretched and vigorously beating the air, came charging towards me. Mature Black Swans spend their lives with only one mate.

The male, which is known as a cob, and the female, referred to as a pen, will both aggressively defend their nest and, having received their message loud and clear, I made a hasty retreat from their domain.

Swans appear rather ungainly as they waddle across dry land but it's a different story when they're on the water, for as they paddle along at a leisurely pace these majestic birds are a picture of elegance and although their efforts to take off from the water seem long and laboured, these great birds, with a wing span of up to two metres, paint an image of true beauty as they fly across the skies.

Swans are herbivores that thrive on a diet that's dominated by aquatic plants and algae and by vegetation that hems the wetlands, rivers and lakes that they inhabit. When feeding in shallow water they simply peer beneath the surface to grab a bite to eat or scoop up floating vegetation, but in other situations it's heads down and bottoms up, with only the birds' tails left high and dry as they gather food from deeper waters.

The loss of natural habitats and the pollution of water sources pose an ongoing threat to populations of Black Swans that, like many other species of waterbirds, have become increasingly accustomed to the presence of humans and domestic dogs. Having subsequently lost their fear of some predators they've become more vulnerable to attacks by feral dogs and foxes, but despite the varied dangers they face, Black Swans, with a lifespan of up to 40 years, are sure to be around for many years to come.

Where you'll find them: These nomadic birds continually search for new areas where there are extensive bodies of water with ample supplies of food. Although they frequent freshwater and saltwater wetlands, rivers and lakes from coastal regions to the outback, they are regular visitors to urban parklands that incorporate large expanses of water or that hem waterways.

Black-winged Stilt

Himantopus himantopus

One September day I was driving along a dusty road near the Queensland outback town of Quilpie on a route that would take me to the isolated settlement of Adavale. The weather, although it was only spring, was hot enough to make even a ragged scarecrow feel a little hot under the collar and my body clock let me know, with niggling pangs of hunger, that it was time for lunch. Fortunately I knew the perfect spot to combine a picnic in a cool and shaded location with some birdwatching and I whispered a plea to whatever gods might be listening. "Please, please don't let the area be congested with noisy campers." Someone, it seemed had been listening to my prayers, for when I arrived at Lake Houdraman, a vast shallow expanse of water hemmed by shading trees, the only sound of life was the squelching footsteps of cattle as they plodded through the muddy edges of the lake to quench their thirst and munch on the succulent grasses that sprouted from the shallow water.

I made myself a sandwich and a cup of coffee and settled down on a log that was merely a few metres from the water's edge with the intention of doing nothing more than admiring the view that, sadly, was devoid of any sign of birds or other wild creatures. The cattle eyed my arrival with

undisguised suspicion and I watched their disgruntled stares as, unimpressed by my presence, they dawdled reluctantly towards the distant grasslands leaving me alone, absorbed by my thoughts and appreciating the solitude and the cooling breeze that drifted across the lake.

I heard no sounds that would herald the arrival of any avian visitors – no chirps or squawks, no flutter of wings, no murmur of disturbed foliage – but suddenly, unexpectedly, the performers who would entertain me while I dined al fresco arrived on the scene as quietly as an army of shuffling centipedes. A bird fluttered down from the sky, then another and then a third, with the little trio of Black-winged Stilts landing in the blue water that lay at the heart of the flat outback landscape with the grace and elegance of butterflies carried on their journey by an almost imperceptible breeze.

Black-winged Stilts, with their stark black-and-white plumage and long red legs, are also known as 'Pied Stilts' and by the colloquial name of 'Longshanks.' They are among the most glamorous and agile of all wading birds. Occasionally they're seen alone but these are usually gregarious birds that prefer to feed in small groups. If there's an abundance of food on offer they come together in large and vociferous flocks to enjoy the bounty that nature has generously provided.

One bird gave a brief and furtive glimpse in my direction and waded across to its companions with a confident and nonchalant expression. "She looks harmless enough," it seemed to say. "Let's just pretend that we haven't seen her and perhaps she'll go away" – but I wasn't going anywhere in a hurry. I was confident that, despite their lack of any rainbow-coloured plumage, these charismatic and slender birds, which strode confidently through the shallow water, would put on a memorable display.

The trio that were to perform for me began the cabaret by dawdling through the water at a pace rivalling that of a gaggle of inebriated barnacles, their eyes focused almost hypnotically on their aquatic environment. Every now and then they plunged their heads beneath the surface of the water in search of the insects and small crustaceans that are a major component of their diet but, with luck appearing to have abandoned them, they opted for another tactic and probed the mud at the water's edge until they were rewarded with miniscule yet nutritious snacks that they gulped down with great enthusiasm.

Suddenly the outback silence was shattered as loud voices and the slamming of car doors announced the arrival of grey nomads who, with their caravan, had begun to set up their temporary home only a few metres away from my waterfront seat.

"Thanks for the captivating show," I whispered as the birds made a hasty exit from the scene and with barely a murmur of their wings, they took to the air and, flying in neat formation, they headed on their way to feast elsewhere. "I'll look forward to seeing you or some of your relatives in the future," I called as they vanished into the distance. Since that memorable day I've encountered Black-winged Stilts in other outback wetlands and in urban parks and every elegant performance has been as mesmerising as the first.

"G'day mate," one of the grey nomads called. "Is there anything to see here?" "Not now," I replied in my most tempered tone. "They've all left for quieter places." "And I hope you'll do the same," I whispered under my breath.

Where you'll find them: These stilts are found throughout the Australian mainland and inhabit a wide range of aquatic environments including freshwater and saltwater wetlands, mudflats and tidal estuaries, in addition to the shallow waters and muddy shores of lakes and rivers.

Nankeen Night Heron

Nycticorax caledonicus

Within minutes of arriving at the sleepy Queensland outback town of Bollon I was wandering along the tree-lined banks of Wallum Creek that's the wild hub of this less than bustling settlement. I peered into every shaded nook and cranny to see what birds might be hiding there but the most attractive of the creek's residents had no need to hide from view among the dense foliage, for with its mottled brown plumage and perched on a leaf-draped branch overhanging the water it was as well camouflaged as a solitary ant at a convention of cockroaches.

"You really are a good-looking fella and that's a magnificent disguise you're wearing," I whispered as the young bird returned my stare of admiration. Young Nankeen Night Herons hide their identity well, for they bear little resemblance to their parents and are so dramatically different that it's often erroneously assumed that immature birds are members of an entirely different species.

The Nankeen Night Heron's name provides a hint of confusion too, for this is a species with behavioural patterns that are unlike those of most other nocturnal birds. For much of the day birds, both young and old, take life as easy as a community of scarecrows on the night shift and doze among the foliage of the trees at the water's edge but during wet or cloudy weather they're often out and about and on the hunt for food during daylight hours, which is exactly what another juvenile bird was doing when I made its acquaintance further west, at the remote opal-mining town of Yowah.

At midday it was sneaking along in the shallow water of a tree-lined stream where warm water from an artesian bore trickled past ramshackle miners' huts. The bird tossed me a momentary scowl that suggested that I should keep my distance to avoid disrupting its hunt for prey, then suddenly, having caught a glimpse of a tiny fish in the algae-laden water, it focused its attentions on the task at hand and, with the speed and accuracy of an Olympic javelin thrower, it snatched its prey with its long pointed bill and strolled on its way to find the second course of its meal.

In Australia's colonial era, early settlers made some of their clothing from a cinnamon-brown fabric called nankeen and with herons that were frequently seen around permanent sources of water having plumage of a similar hue, the birds were ultimately christened with a name that

readily identified them. They became known as Nankeen Night Herons but it's only adult birds that wear any distinctive cinnamon brown attire.

One winter's day, as dusk approached, I spotted an adult night heron relaxing beside the Bulloo River near the outback town of Thargomindah. It reluctantly stirred from its slumber and fluttered down to the river's perpetually muddy waters to hunt for any small crustaceans, fish, frogs or aquatic insects that would satisfy its hunger. The long streamers of narrow white feathers adorning its black crown indicated that, in addition to the essential need for food, it had the prospect of mating and starting a new family on its mind. Its offspring would be well camouflaged with the dark and mottled plumage of the young birds that I had previously encountered and, for a considerable time, would resemble their parents as much as a slab of granite resembles a slice of mouldy gruyere cheese.

I've often needed a hefty serving of patience to discover a Nankeen Night Heron as it sits, silently, in its daytime retreat but every glimpse of this attractive bird, in whatever dress it's been wearing, has provided a memorable experience and I'm keeping my fingers crossed that my most recent encounter won't be my last.

Where you'll find them: Woodlands and forests on the banks of waterways, lakes, coastal estuaries and freshwater swamps throughout mainland Australia are the favoured haunts of Nankeen Night Herons. These birds are occasionally seen in similar environments in Tasmania.

Pacific Black Duck

Anas superciliosa

These waterbirds are as familiar to many people as tomato sauce and burnt snags at an Aussie barbecue. Known to everyone simply as 'ducks', they're the birds that children delight in feeding in urban parks, when both youngsters and wildfowl seem to gain equal pleasure from the encounter.

Anas, the name of the genus to which this aquatic bird belongs, is a Latin word that simply means 'duck' but it's also an Arabic word meaning 'friendly' and that's a most appropriate description of the Pacific Black Duck that always appreciates a free meal.

As a child I fed the ducks that visited a local park and I've admired them ever since. "But it's just a duck!" my other half exclaims disparagingly whenever I become excited at the sight of one or more of these charming birds but familiarity fails to diminish my passion for these charismatic characters.

Many Pacific Black Ducks happily spend the majority of their lives in urban environments, but others continue to live a truly wild existence and, being able to thrive wherever there's sufficient water and a reliable supply of food, they're as content to paddle on the calm waters of rivers, lakes, and wetlands as they are on parkland ponds, irrigation canals and farm dams. I've seen them in countless locations, from coastal regions to the most remote corners of the outback, but one rural encounter stands out from every other chance meeting with these most common of waterbirds.

I'd set up camp beside the picturesque Tooloom Falls in northern New South Wales and on a cold and miserable winter's morning I reluctantly crawled out of my sleeping bag as dawn hinted that the weather would not be improving. A grey mist hung low among the surrounding forests, raindrops splashed into muddy puddles and the icy hand of a gentle breeze sent me hurrying back inside for an additional layer of warm clothing. Just the weather for ducks I thought and right on cue, as I peered beyond the gaping door of my tent, a pair of Pacific Black Ducks waddled past.

They bravely dabbled in the puddles, nibbled at blades of grass that bowed low as though cowering before the irate gods of weather, dawdled across a carpet of rocks towards the high precipice over which the waters of Tooloom Creek tumbled and stood staring at the stunning view as though contemplating their next adventure. "Go on jump!" I taunted them. "I dare you!" They leant forward, peering over the edge with the same hint of unease that I felt when I ventured a little too close. "Go on, jump – or fly!" I urged them but they couldn't be persuaded and waddled off through the drizzling rain, dabbling in the ice-coated puddles among the rocks, fluttering their dark brown feathers to wash themselves in the light rain and finally wandered back to the creek to hunt for some scrumptious breakfast snacks.

Pacific Black Ducks feed primarily on aquatic plants and supplement their diet with insects, small crustaceans and water snails that they catch by briefly plunging their heads beneath the water with only their tails protruding from the surface, a posture that has earned them the title of 'dabbling ducks.'

I'd been forced to retreat from weather that had left me feeling as miserable as a sewerage worker with a rat up his trousers, but after thawing out with a hot cuppa and some breakfast

I headed back outside to renew my acquaintance with the ducks.

Having clambered onto a solitary rock in the midst of the narrow stream they were taking life at a pace equalling that of a wandering winkle on a day out in a sand dune and were doing nothing more energetic than preened their plumage. Welcome rays of sunlight that speared through the retreating clouds illuminated the patch of iridescent green feathers on each bird's wings and as they glinted, like dazzling jewels, among the ducks' predominantly brown plumage the birds slipped silently into the water and paddled slowly upstream into the shadows of the surrounding forest, leaving me alone with indelible memories of a brief yet delightful encounter.

"What have you been watching?" my other half enquired when he eventually joined me beside the creek. "Nothing unusual," I replied. "Just some ducks."

Where you'll find them: Pacific Black Ducks can be found in all but the most arid regions of Australia with their habitats including any expanse of water, from a small and isolated pool to tidal mudflats, sprawling wetlands, lakes and rivers.

Australian Pelican

Pelecanus conspicillatus

Only a glut of adjectives could accurately describe the Australian Pelican and affable, handsome, graceful and intelligent can only just begin to paint a true picture of this most familiar of aquatic birds. Despite all its positive attributes there's one characteristic that many people fail to associate with the seemingly placid pelican. It can be aggressive too, and when, as a child, I first saw a flock of these large birds in the parklands in the South Australian city of Adelaide, there was plenty of argy bargy going on.

Pacific Black Ducks, Black Swans and Silver Gulls were clamouring for free handouts of bread but when a squadron of pelicans strode onto the scene smaller birds had to accept a lower place in the pecking order while the big and bossy characters received the lion's share of the feast.

Since that day I've encountered pelicans on many occasions. I've watched them drifting at a leisurely pace on lakes, rivers and streams. I've seen them on beaches and beside boat ramps and jetties where they plead for fishermen's scraps and squabble among themselves to snatch whatever treats are tossed their way. And I've met them in the outback too, for wherever there's water and

thus the chance of catching fish that are the major ingredient of their diet pelicans are as happy as blowflies in a dustbin.

I once assumed that pelicans, although they'll argue over food, were gentle giants that meant no one any harm but that opinion was abruptly shattered one winter's day when I was paddling my kayak on the calm waters of a river hemmed by the forests of Victoria's Croajingolong National Park.

A small flock of pelicans that was lazing on the shores of a low and sandy island created an idyllic scene of wildlife relaxing, but as I paddled slowly towards the bank it was obvious that I was far from welcome. With every bird alerted to my approach the boss cocky of the gang, stretching itself up to its full height and with its great wings outstretched, charged towards me at a terrifying speed. Its message was clear. This was the domain of pelicans alone and my presence was definitely not appreciated. "I'm not one of the bad guys mate and I mean you no harm, so you don't need to get your knickers in a twist or your tail in a tangle," I mumbled as I made a hasty retreat in the

face of the bird's continuing threat of attack and it eventually waddled back to its companions, proudly flaunting its success at deterring an armada of one, while continually maintaining a wary eye on my location.

After one intimidating encounter I made it a rule to always keep well away from pelicans and on the banks of Cooper Creek, near the South Australian outback town of Innamincka, I stood beyond the danger zone as a squadron of these imposing birds demonstrated their indisputable skills at fishing. Pelicans often feed alone but on this occasion a group of mates were fishing together and appeared as happy in their work as a swarm of dung beetles in a fresh dollop of manure.

The pouch attached to a pelican's bill is extremely sensitive and it's this sensitivity that allows the birds to find their prey even in water that resembles the thickest and most unpalatable pea soup. As I watched from a discreet distance the birds instinctively formed an arc to surround their prey that they then herded into the shallow water at the creek's muddy edge. Finally, with a meal within their reach, they plunged their bills into the water and, using their pouches as nets, they scooped up their catch. The reward for their efforts was a large fish for some, yet nothing for others and for those that had missed out the battle was on. With the flapping of dozens of wings the birds fought to either steal or retain a meal and as the once calm waters of the creek were whipped to muddy foam I was pleased to be well away from the conflict.

There was no hint of aggression among the small number of pelicans that I later encountered at the sleepy settlement of Baird Bay on South Australia's Eyre Peninsula. The leisurely lifestyle of fishermen who call the village home seemed to be contagious and I watched Pacific Gulls and pelicans drifting lazily on the calm blue waters that lapped at the beach while others loitered beside the boat ramp with the knowledge that any returning fisherman might offer them a free snack, I emulated their less than energetic mood.

Well beyond the shore there was a disaster unfolding however, and I watched in dismay as a pelican attempted to devour a piece of floating plastic. An estimated eight million tonnes of rubbish, much of which is plastic, is dumped into the world's oceans every year, and seabirds, mistakenly identifying this debris as food, frequently ingest it. Today around half of all seabirds have some plastic in their gut that may eventually lead to their death and with the prediction that, by 2050, some 95 per cent of all seabirds will become the victims of plastic, the future looks very grim indeed.

The pelican was too far from the shore for me to attempt to save it from what might have been a lingering death but as I considered what if any action I could take a fisherman in a dilapidated dinghy puttered into view, fracturing the calm surface of the water and allowing fate to intervene and chase the pelican to the skies, abandoning what it had erroneously assumed would be an easy meal.

Pelicans are one of the heaviest flying birds in the world but with a wingspan of around 2.5 metres they make the art of flight seem effortless and can glide and soar for extensive periods of time. They routinely fly at altitudes of around 1,000 metres, with some adventurous birds reaching the breathtaking height of 3,000 metres. With relief that one bird had been spared from the scourge of plastic I watched in awe as it captured the spiralling thermals that carried it from what could have been hell on earth to the safety of the skies.

Where you'll find them: Australian Pelicans, with a population of between 300,000 and 500,000 individuals, can be found almost anywhere where there is water – from coastal beaches, estuaries and harbours to inland rivers, lakes and wetlands, and to the most remote corners of the outback.

Australian Darter

Anhinga novaehollandiae

At the Tondoon Botanic Gardens in the Queensland city of Gladstone I've often spent a leisurely hour or two dining on the deck above the water of a lake that's hemmed by forests and that's a focal point for many aquatic birds. From here I've frequently had a bird's-eye view of the darter in action.

It's a bird that revels in its own company and that seeks out others of its kind only when it's nudged into becoming more sociable by the urge to breed. In countless places, I've watched it feed on aquatic plants and search for prey that includes insects and crustaceans as it meanders, at little more than the speed of a rampaging mob of turtles, along the banks of coastal rivers and outback streams. There's nothing slow and slothful about the darter once it enters the water however, for it's here that it demonstrates its unrivalled skills as a predator.

When it's in hunting mode and with a feast of fish on its mind it glides effortlessly through the water with no part of its anatomy visible other than its long snake-like neck that has earned this graceful bird the alternative names of 'Snakebird' and 'Snake-necked Darter'. When its prey comes into view the darter skilfully spears its victim with its sharp and pointed bill.

Darters, when they're in their aquatic environment, are elusive characters for they're here

one minute and gone the next. I often attempt to guess where, after a bird has vanished beneath the water, it will ultimately resurface and I'm invariably wrong for these amazing birds have the ability to remain submerged for a considerable length of time and pop up again where they're least expected.

They have dramatically different lifestyles to many other aquatic birds that are endowed with waterproof feathers to guarantee them the buoyancy they require to float on the surface of the water. A high degree of buoyancy is certainly not on the darter's wish list however for these are birds that generally claim the bottom of shallow streams and lakes as their dining table and too much buoyancy would make their lives intolerable.

When a darter has finally sated its appetite it takes life easy for a while as it perches on a sunlit tree stump or an old post beside the water with its wings stretched out to dry – it then becomes as conspicuous as an emu in a hen house. "Was the fishing good today?" I sometimes enquire of a bird that's in its most iconic pose and I wish, for a fleeting moment, that if reincarnation was to be my destiny I would be reborn as a waterbird and emulate the enviable aquatic skills of a darter.

One warm and sunny winter's day my attention was captured by a darter that was standing motionlessly on a log at the edge of a lagoon near the Queensland outback town of Clermont and when I heard a muted chirp I realised that the bird was not alone. Three large and fluffy chicks,

crammed into a ragged nest of sticks that had been constructed on a branch overhanging the water, were becoming more than a little agitated as they waited for a parent to deliver their next meal. They jostled for a position that each hoped would guarantee them the attention of the adult that was doing its best to ignore its pleading brood. Each came precariously close to the rim of the nest as they stretched their long necks out and noisily demanded food and parental attention.

"Stay where you are fellas! Stop! Stop! Don't take another step!" I whispered in panic in the hope that Mother Nature would take control of the situation and nudge the chicks back from the brink of disaster and save them from tumbling into the water and to their inevitable death – and she played her role of nanny admirably. The adult, perhaps sensing that trouble was brewing, began fluttering and leaping upwards in an ungainly fashion and finally managed to tumble into the nest. "Now what do you lot think you were doing? I told you to sit still and behave yourselves!" it seemed to say as it admonished the young birds that had been almost too adventurous for their own good. As the little family snuggled up together and settled down to doze I prayed that the chicks would all survive to enjoy the amazing aquatic life that lay ahead of them.

Where you'll find them: The darter is found in most areas of the Australian mainland wherever there are suitably large bodies of water such as freshwater lakes and wetlands.

Straw-necked Ibis

Threskiornis spinicollis

"Good morning! Is that really you Mister Ibis?" I said when, paddling my kayak along the Ward River in outback Queensland, I noticed a large black bird, with its back towards me, perched on the railings of a disused bridge. It cautiously turned its head in my direction and I knew, the moment its eyes met mine, that I'd made a faux pas of monumental proportions, at least as far as the bird was concerned. Now don't get me wrong, I'm not a mind reader and I'm certainly not fluent in any avian dialect but I know a dirty look when I'm on the receiving end of one. The Straw-necked Ibis appeared unimpressed by my comments and it might have been my use of the name 'ibis' that had hit a nerve. "You can pick your friends but not your family," the bird's haughty stare seemed to say, "and although I'm a close relative of the Australian Ibis, don't you dare to associate me with those uncouth creatures." And who could blame this beautiful bird for wanting to disassociate itself from its white city cousins that are commonly known as 'rubbish dump chooks' and 'tip turkeys?'

The mere mention of an ibis often conjures up images of these large birds that have made themselves as welcome in urban areas as a swarm of ravenous weevils in a rice pudding. Immense flocks not only gather in parklands but also forage for food in rubbish tips and wherever they live and whatever they're doing Australian Ibises are undeniably slobs of the first order with their plumage invariably unkempt and dirty.

"Anyone with an IQ higher than that of a dung beetle could see that I'm far superior to them in every respect," the Straw-necked Ibis seemed to say as it turned around and glared in my direction with its head held high in a haughty pose. With the straw-like feathers that are the reason for its common name conspicuously protruding from its neck and its immaculate black feathers glinting in the early morning sunshine I had no hesitation in apologising for any unintended insult. "No one could deny that you really are the most beautiful ibis," I said as it slowly stretched its wings, gracefully launched itself into the air and flew downstream, following the river's tree-lined course.

I resumed my own journey and paddled along the river at a leisurely pace, keeping one eye on the jumble of rocks that protruded from the water and the other on the bird as it soared with the ease and grace of a snowflake dancing to the tune of a gentle breeze. Straw-necked Ibises are nomadic birds and frequently fly vast distances across the continent on journeys that are prompted

primarily by seasonal conditions and the eternal search for food. I imagined that the bird I had met was perhaps undertaking a new adventure and might challenge the record-breaking flight of one of its species that had covered a distance of more than 3,500 kilometres on an epic journey from the south-western corner of the continent to south-eastern Queensland. I silently wished it bon voyage as it rounded a bend in the river and vanished from sight.

A little later, further downstream, I clambered up the riverbank and beyond its cloak of trees hoping to discover other outback birds. The sprawling plains that lay beyond the river were saturated with water after heavy overnight rain and as I emerged from the shadows of the trees a hundred faces turned to see who had intruded into their domain and a hundred pairs of wings beat the air as a flock of Straw-necked Ibises momentarily became airborne. Then, realising that I posed no threat, every bird settled back down to probe the sodden ground with their long curved bills and continue the hunt for tasty snacks. Grasshoppers and locusts are among their favoured foods but Straw-necked Ibises will also eat frogs, small reptiles, mammals and even mice. Unlike their cousin, the Australian Ibis, they prefer life in the great outdoors rather than in urban areas and among this feasting flock there was not a dirty bird to be seen.

Where you'll find them: These ibises are most at home in grasslands and in areas that are close to wetlands. They can be seen throughout Australia although they are rarely found on coastal shores and are generally absent from the most arid inland regions..

White-faced Heron

Egretta novaehollandiae

I've seen them here, I've seen them there, in fact I've seen White-faced Herons almost everywhere – from the coast to the outback. This is the most common species of heron in Australia and wherever there's either freshwater or salt water, even if it's only a relatively small pool, there's a good chance that one of these elegant wading birds won't be too far away.

My first encounter with a White-faced Heron was at the Ward River that mutters through bushland near the Queensland outback town of Charleville. I was travelling and camping alone

and taking life at a relaxed pace rivalling that of a skeleton in a medical student's wardrobe and that's exactly what White-faced Herons often do.

These are birds that generally live alone and that frequently demonstrate as much activity as mould creeping across a slice of last week's bread as they wait patiently for unsuspecting prey to come their way or simply dawdle along the muddy banks of a river or a murky stream in search of a snack. The individual that was on my doorstep was employing a slightly more energetic tactic in its efforts to locate a meal however. It strolled, step by slowly calculated step, tiptoeing silently through the water, stopping every now and then to use its large feet to stir mud and water into a murky soup in the hope of flushing any fish or crustaceans out of their aquatic retreats. As each doomed creature made a frenetic dash for survival, the heron, with its great wings outstretched, charged off in pursuit at a speed rivalling that of a frenzied gecko covered in meat ants, with only creatures granted immunity by Lady Luck able to escape the bird's predatory attentions.

There was more rock than either mud or water in the meandering creek where a White-faced Heron had taken up residence among the forested ranges near the New South Wales town of Eden, but even in this confined and narrow waterway the bird's hunting tactics mirrored those of its outback cousins. I settled down on a log where I assumed that I'd be discreetly concealed among the boulders and the shadows of the forest's tangled vegetation but few signs of life escape the attentions of these herons. "Don't let me disrupt your leisurely life," I whispered as the bird gave a disapproving glare in my direction but realising that I posed no imminent threat it decided to ignore me.

The brownish-grey feathers, known as nuptial plumes, that adorned the bird's head, neck, and back were a clear sign that it was in the mood for love but it also had food on its mind and stood motionlessly in a shallow pool, appreciating the warming fingers of sunshine that clawed through a gap in the forest canopy on a chilly winter's day, waiting for any movement in the water that trickled seductively past its feet. Suddenly it burst into action with speed and bravado as it rushed forward, stabbing at the water in a frenzied attack, stabbing here, there and everywhere within its reach but with nothing to show for its efforts the bird demonstrated a look of utter frustration. "You need to hone your skills a bit mate if you expect to survive," I mumbled as the bird stared in my direction. "Perhaps you should just ignore me and concentrate on what you're doing." "What would you know?" the bird's gaze seemed to say and as if to prove that it was a highly accomplished predator it whipped around, grabbed a tiny creature from the water with incredible speed and accuracy and gulped down the tasty morsel before resuming its patient wait for another easy meal, for any frog, small reptile or insect that ventured into nature's cafeteria.

Where you'll find them: White-faced Herons can be seen in any region of the continent where there is a source of water and make themselves at home in a wide range of habitats. These include beaches, tidal mudflats, river estuaries, coastal and outback wetlands and other waterways. They are often seen meandering across wet grasslands and pastures and in urban parklands that have appropriate sources of water.

White-necked Heron

Ardea pacifica

The perpetually muddy Paroo River that slices through the often arid landscape of south-western Queensland is an important resource, not only for human residents of the outback but also for wildlife. It was on the river's wooded banks that I first encountered a White-necked Heron and it was doing absolutely nothing to attract my attention. It was perched on the railings of a bridge near the tiny settlement of Eulo and this attractive bird, which is also known as a Pacific Heron,

was simply watching travellers come and go within such close proximity that its feathers were ruffled by the breeze of each passing vehicle. As I drove slowly past I was confident that, if I had wound down the window, I could have reached out and touched the bird's silken feathers, yet it remained motionless and unperturbed by my presence. "I bet you'd spring into action if a fish was to swim your way!" I called out as the heron's stern gaze followed mine but it remained in its rigid position as though silently guarding the entrance to the sleepy township.

White-necked Herons were also at home on the banks of the Ward River that hides among bushland near the outback town of Charleville and after I'd set up camp on the riverbank I launched my kayak that would allow me to drift silently, stealthily along the river and sneak a peek at any creatures that might be out and about. Galahs, Pied Cormorants and Straw-necked Ibises were all in the vicinity but it was a bird in the distance, a bird perched on a dead tree, that caught my attention with its curious pose and its wings wrapped around its body like a comforting shawl.

Despite my lack of camouflage and with my bright orange kayak and vivid yellow life jacket ensuring that I was as conspicuous as a shark in a goldfish pond, the juvenile White-necked Heron,

with its distinctive grey-and-white streaked plumage, barely glanced in my direction as, propelled on my way by only the river's feeble current, I drifted slowly downstream. The young bird squawked as I passed and followed my arrival and subsequent departure with a stare that reflected curiosity more than fear. As it squawked again, an adult heron further downstream, alerted to the call of what might have been its offspring, tentatively prepared to flee.

I paddled slowly and quietly towards the bank, tied my kayak to a tree trunk and crept discreetly through the river's cloak of bushland to get a better view of the heron that, rather than retreat, had dived into the water and caught a fish. I muttered what my mother used to say when I wanted the largest piece of cake on the tray, "Your eyes are too big for your stomach," for herons, unlike raptors, cannot rip their prey to pieces but must swallow it whole and this fish was far too big for any heron to consume.

The fish, desperate to survive, wriggled and squirmed in the heron's bill and finally escaped from its captor but it was out of the frying pan and into the fire for the doomed creature. I watched the drama unfold, saw the fish writhing on the muddy bank only inches from the safety of the water and silently cheered it on in its struggle for survival – until a Whistling Kite dived from the sky and snatched it in its talons. The fish, continuing to struggle, slipped from the raptor's tenacious grasp – only to be snapped up by the heron once again before making yet another miraculous escape. The kite, still intent on obtaining an easy meal, once again grabbed the fish from the riverbank and again the aquatic Houdini escaped – only to have another raptor, one that appeared from nowhere, arrive on the scene and successful carry its prey away.

I applauded the tenacity of the fish and was saddened by its demise but every bird has to eat and for the White-necked Heron it was back to square one in the hunt for food. These are birds that demonstrate interminable patience as they wait in silence at the water's edge or wade in the shallows in search of prey that includes not only fish but also frogs, crustaceans and aquatic insects, and when they spot a potential meal they strike with lightning speed. "Better luck next time mate and don't be so greedy in future" I called across the river as the bird once again focused its attention on the river's murky water.

Where you'll find them: The White-necked Heron is found in most regions of Australia, although it's seldom seen in Tasmania or in coastal areas. Its favoured habitats are freshwater wetlands, shallow lakes and waterways, including those of outback regions.

Yellow-billed Spoonbill

Platalea flavipes

When I arrived at the remote Coongie Lakes National Park in outback South Australia I expected to see water and consequently to meet several species of birds, but what I hadn't anticipated was a wetland so extensive that it appeared like a vast inland sea.

I trudged across a sprawling expanse of sand that, after light rain, was daubed with an astounding diversity of wildflowers and as I reached the lake that stretched to every distant

horizon I was greeted by a cacophony of honking and splashing as a flock of pelicans fled from the scene. Masked Plovers, less concerned by my arrival, strolled across the damp sand at the water's edge as Whistling Kites twirled and danced on the discreet breezes of an azure sky but it was a less familiar bird that caught my attention as it strode through the calm blue water, one hesitant step at a time, at a pace replicating that of a three-legged tortoise on broken crutches. "Good morning!" I whispered so quietly that only I could hear my voice and the Yellow-billed Spoonbill, glancing nonchalantly in my direction for less than a fragment of a second, continued its search for prey.

It's the shape of the bird's bill that has given this species its common name but who ever saw a spoon of such immense proportions? The cutlery with which the Yellow-billed Spoonbill scoops up its food is slightly smaller than the bill of its close relative the Royal Spoonbill but the inside of the bill has the same sensors that enable every bird to detect the movement of even the tiniest creatures in the surrounding water. I watched in silent awe as the large white bird slowly moved its bill from side to side through the water in search of any small fish, aquatic insects and crustaceans, such as yabbies, that would make a substantial meal and I made no sound or movement until, continually and rhythmically sifting the water through its perfectly designed bill, it waded into the distance.

Several weeks later, from a well-concealed spot beneath the gnarled trees that cast their shadows over Eyre Creek, south of the Queensland outback town of Birdsville, I had a front-row seat for another entertaining performance by a small group of Yellow-billed Spoonbills. Each was focusing so intently on the search for food that they remained oblivious to my presence as they patrolled among the forest of reeds that hemmed the water's edge. "I know there's food in this creek and by crikey I'm going to get it even if I have to wade through the water for as long as it would take a three-legged echidna to scale the heights of Everest," one bird, with a stoic expression of determination, seemed to say. It shuffled along faster than its companions, scooping its great bill in a wider arc through the water – left, right, left, right, scoop, shuffle, scoop, shuffle – as though attempting to impress the other birds with its stamina and dexterity. With its efforts receiving attention only from me, the bird strode through the reeds and stepped out onto the stream's wooded bank. It fluffed up its feathers and preened itself in an attempt to impress its mates but they continued to demonstrate as much interest as I might show in a sackful of desiccated earwigs.

"Your mates might not think that you're particularly attractive but you've certainly impressed me," I whispered as the spoonbill continued its attempt to attract attention. "And who asked for your opinion?" its glare of derision implied. "What you think is not of importance to me." Having put me firmly in my place, the great bird arrogantly strode back into the murky water to resume the hunt for its elusive prey.

Every Yellow-billed Spoonbill, with its pale yellow face, long legs and unique bill, is an unmistakable character but this bird, keen to attract a mate for the coming breeding season, had

added a little bling to its attire and with lacy plumes tipped with black on the edges of its wings it was unquestionably, at least for me, the star attraction at the remote and tranquil corner of the outback that, for a moment in time, it called its home.

Where you'll find them: Yellow-billed Spoonbills are more selective in regard to their habitat than their closest relative the Royal Spoonbill and although they're found in many aquatic environments across the continent, particularly in freshwater wetlands and lakes in northern and inland areas, they are rarely seen in the saltwater wetlands of coastal regions.

Black-fronted Dotterel

Elseyornis melanops

The Black-fronted Dotterel is unquestionably the most charming of small birds. I could spend countless hours watching this attractive and hyperactive little character and I've done just that on many occasions in locations that range from the outback to parklands within busy coastal cities.

"It's your turn to make tea tonight," my other half reminded me as I wandered from our campsite towards a shallow lake near the outback Queensland town of Eulo. "Don't worry, I'll be back in plenty of time," I replied but that was before I met the Black-fronted Dotterel and became captivated by its energetic activities.

Some people refer to this enchanting little bird as a 'guttersnipe' and I'm insulted on its behalf for my dictionary defines a guttersnipe as 'a young, uncared for and mischievous child.' That's certainly not an apt description of a bird that's invariably dressed in immaculately clean plumage and whose behaviour includes nothing more mischievous than the fun of dabbling about in the mud that hems the lakes and wetlands that are its favoured habitats.

Small is certainly beautiful in this bird's case and although the Black-fronted Dotterel's attire is a splendid example of Mother Nature's unparalleled artistic skills, she's also provided the little fella with plumage that guarantees that it's always well camouflaged on the grey-brown mud that surrounds the aquatic areas that it frequents. Indeed it was only when it made a sudden and hasty move that I was alerted to its presence.

This dotterel is a hyperactive little bundle of energy that, for a while, dawdles across the mud at little more than the pace of a centipede with 100 arthritic knees, peck, peck, pecking at the ground as though perhaps eating one minute insect after another. It's a different story however when more substantial prey appears and the tiny bird rushes at high speed in pursuit of its quarry and momentarily savours its snack before resuming its leisurely stroll. "I wish I had a fraction of your energy mate," I whispered enviously as I watched the tiny bird's repetitious stop-start activities, but it had no time to be disrupted by my idle chatter and rushed on its way to grab another insect from the mud or some barely visible aquatic creature from the lake's shallowest water.

Black-fronted Dotterels often spend their days with a mate but even when they're on their own, which is frequently the case, they appear as happy as termites in the rotting timbers of an outback dunny. Far from the dust of the outback, at central Queensland's picturesque Eungella Dam, I watched a solitary dotterel scurrying along the water's edge and hunting for its prey among the floating leaves of waterlilies. It came to a sudden standstill as it noticed my arrival on the scene and stood motionlessly in the shallow water as though the lack of movement granted it invisibility. I applied the same logic to my activities and it worked, for the little bird resumed its frenetic pace, rushing here and rushing there through mud, shallow water and lily leaves.

A small flock of these tiny birds was in action at the Fitzroy River west of the city of Rockhampton too, dabbling among rocky pools and rushing in every direction in search of food. "Good luck with your hunting," I muttered as I cautiously crept along the river's forested bank "but don't forget that this is a dangerous place to be." There was danger here for both birds and birdwatcher, for the Fitzroy River is inhabited by crocodiles and when a bird of prey rose from the water's edge with a screech of alarm I was reminded of the need to keep an eye out for the most fearful of predators and not to focus my attentions entirely on the entertaining antics of the Black-fronted Dotterel.

Where you'll find them: These small shorebirds are found in all but the most arid regions of the country. They occasionally inhabit coastal mudflats and river estuaries but their preference is for freshwater wetlands and lakes, in addition to the shallow pools of water that fill outback claypans. As a ground-dwelling species these charming little birds are vulnerable to predation by feral cats and foxes and with long and repetitive droughts having a severe impact on wetlands and shallow bodies of water, life has become less than easy for Black-fronted Dotterels and their populations are in decline in some regions.

Brolga

Grus rubicunda

As I rolled into a waterfront camping area at the sleepy western Queensland town of Bollon that dozes on the banks of Wallum Creek the town's residents and the Koalas that inhabit the adjacent woodlands were taking it easy but there was frenetic activity in the dead centre of the settlement. Two Brolgas, birds that stand approximately two metres high, were performing their mesmerising dance among the adjacent cemetery's toppled tombstones and I was tempted to believe that they were performing for no other reason than to celebrate my arrival.

An Aboriginal legend tells of a beautiful girl named Buralga who loved to dance but when she rejected the amorous attentions of an evil sorcerer the villain of the story took his revenge and transformed her into a bird. She became a Brolga and Brolgas have retained not only their legendary ancestor's beauty and elegance but also her passion for dancing.

I stood in reverent awe as the birds continued their complex dance routine, silently applauding as one bird pulled some grass from the ground, hurled it into the air and skilfully caught it in its bill while, with its great wings outstretched, it continued its mesmerising dance. It leapt, almost in slow motion, into the air, bowed gracefully to its partner and bobbed its head up and down to the accompaniment of a cacophony of curious calls. "Thanks for the wonderful entertainment mate," I murmured as the display finally came to its conclusion and the birds, striding slowly towards the adjacent woodlands, turned momentarily to glance back in my direction with each bird acknowledging my appreciation with a subtle nod of its head as if to say "We're so pleased that you enjoyed the show."

Brolgas are faithful and monogamous birds and although they spend much of the year with only their mate and other members of their small and close-knit family group as their companions they need no other audience to encourage them to put on an entertaining display at any time of the year. A bird will dance to demonstrate to its mate that it's the most beautiful and elegant of nature's many glamorous creatures. Others will spontaneously join in and as the breeding season approaches and the birds congregate in large flocks the dance becomes an integral part of a complex courtship ritual.

It was the daily necessities of life that were foremost in the minds of the Brolgas that I encountered further west, beyond the far from bustling outback town of Boulia, for here a pair of birds was dawdling along a riverbed at little more than the speed of a hobbled sloth. They seemed oblivious to my presence as they nibbled on the leaves of succulent plants and quietly sipped from the murky water of a shallow pool. As I edged closer, concealed from view by a cluster of trees and low vegetation, I stumbled on the rocky terrain and the yelp of anguish that I omitted as I crashed to the ground sent the birds into panic mode. "Sorry to scare you," I said quietly and as I glanced up from the ground, grimacing in agony, the birds fled to the skies in a display of aerial ballet that was as elegant and captivating as their terrestrial dance and, for a moment, the spectacle obliterated any hint of physical pain quicker than the most powerful analgesic.

The Brolga, which is also known colloquially as the 'Australian Crane' and 'Native Companion,' is the official bird emblem of Queensland and is featured on the state's coat of arms, but such iconic status has failed to provide these great birds with the protection they deserve. The ongoing destruction of their habitat and the presence of feral cats and foxes that devour both the birds' eggs and their vulnerable chicks have led to a dramatic reduction in the Brolgas' population, particularly in the southern extremities of their range, although with their numbers estimated to be between 20,000 and 100,000 birds they're in no imminent danger of extinction.

I've been fortunate to encounter these elegant creatures not only in the outback but also in close proximity to the central Queensland coast where a small flock was striding confidently through grasses at the edge of wetlands. Here they could feast on seeds, roots and succulent leaves with crustaceans, frogs and small lizards on offer as a second course that would certainly give them something pleasurable to dance about. I was happy too, as once again I could admire their performance from a front-row seat.

Where you'll find them: Although Brolgas are most prominent in northern and north-eastern Australia they can also be seen in semi-arid inland regions of the continent and their range extends south to central New South Wales and western Victoria. With a preference for areas close to sources of water, their favoured habitats are wetlands, coastal mudflats, grassy plains and irrigated farmlands.

Bush Stone-curlew

Burhinus grallarius

On a summer's day, when the temperature was hot enough to make even an ageing scarecrow feel a little under the weather, I wasn't the only one taking life easy as I picnicked in the forests of the Kroombit Tops National Park in central Queensland. It was here that I first met the curious Bush Stone-curlew that, with two of its mates, was as in as lively a mood as a gravy-soaked dumpling in a pot of boiling stew.

It was relaxing, squatting down and unperturbed by children playing nearby and vehicles rattling past on the rough and dusty road, for such things, the bird obviously assumed, posed no more of a threat than a leaf floating lazily in a muddy puddle. It was spot on with that assumption, for no one other than I was aware of its existence as it remained camouflaged among a russet carpet of fallen leaves beneath a shading tree.

Eventually, glancing my way with one partially opened golden eye, it began a game that replicated the childhood pastime of musical chairs. It moved slowly, cautiously repositioning one long leg at a time, almost in slow motion, then, the moment I too made a barely visible and hesitant move it stopped abruptly and stood rigidly in whatever peculiar pose it had been in when it remembered that it needed to remain invisible. With its attire of streaked brown plumage it blended into the environment as perfectly as Mother Nature had intended it to.

"I can see you but you can't see me," came the unspoken message as the bird stared at me in rigid silence. "But I'll pose for you if you don't give me away. Do you like this pose, or would you prefer this one?" it seemed to ask as it moved tentatively to perform one statuesque pose after another.

The Bush Stone-curlew is a bird that looks as though it was constructed by an amateur designer using a mish-mash of whatever components were on hand, for it has a long bullet-shaped body that's often carried horizontally on gangly long legs with thick knees – its alternative name is Bush Thick-knee – and a long neck that terminates with a face with large eyes that give a perpetually supercilious stare.

Whenever they feel threatened these curious birds hold their wings out and make a hissing sound. As a boy with a panting dog on a leash came its way the bird showed what it could do while its mates, still in an almost comatose state, dozed on, oblivious to the world around them. "I'm sorry to disappoint you mate but you don't look any scarier than a gang of geriatric centipedes on roller skates," I whispered to the bird as neither the dog nor its owner paid any heed to its display and, with the presumed threat having passed, the bird calmly folded its wings and resumed its motionless stance.

It's only when a more serious threat presents itself that Bush Stone-Curlews, in panic mode, take what, for them, is an extreme course of action and fly into the sky. Their excuse for being as lethargic as a pod of beached whales during daylight hours is that they are primarily a nocturnal species and rarely dawdle into action before the setting sun slithers down beyond the horizon. It's then that they prowl across the ground in the hunt for food and no one could accuse Bush Stone-curlews of being fussy eaters. Frogs, spiders, insects, crustaceans, small snakes and tiny lizards are all integral components of their diet and they'll also devour seeds and succulent roots if that's the best that's on offer.

"I'll leave you to doze in peace," I murmured to the sedentary bird "but perhaps you'll be in a more amorous and active mood next time we meet," I added. What I really wanted to see was the Bush Stone-curlew's courtship dance during which, with its wings and neck outstretched, it stamps its feet up and down rhythmically to some unheard tune. It's a ritual that, to the accompaniment of loud calls, is repeated on and on for an hour or more until the bird attracts the attention of a prospective mate and I look forward to some unique entertainment when next I encounter this curious character.

Where you'll find them: This bird's extensive range covers the majority of the Australian mainland, with the exception of the western coast and much of the arid interior. It's relatively common in tropical and subtropical regions of Queensland but rarely seen in New South Wales and Victoria, where it was once common but is now regarded as endangered. Its habitat includes open forests and eucalyptus woodlands but it will be just as content to live on grassy plains, in dry scrubland and among the vegetation that lines inland watercourses and will even take up residence in urban areas if the vegetation is to its liking..

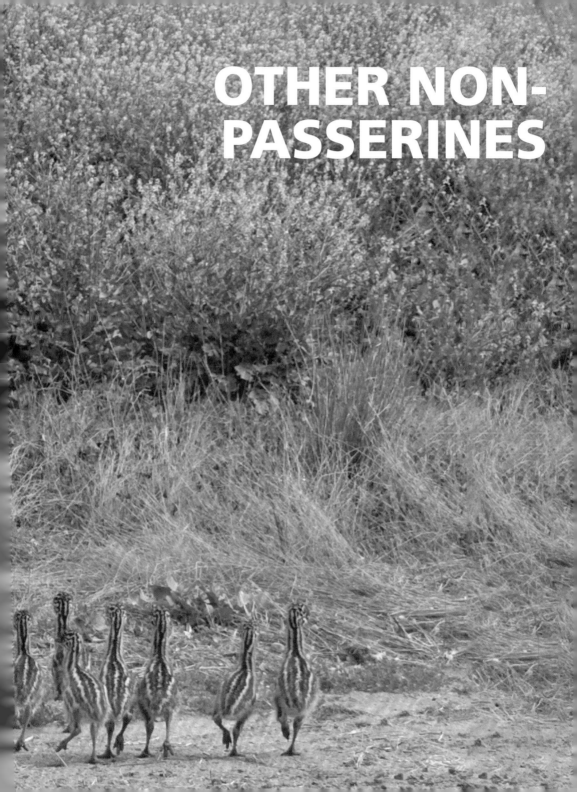

OTHER NON-PASSERINES

Australian Bustard

Ardeotis australis

If I'd been born generations ago and been one of the early European settlers of this vast continent I'd probably have commented on what a good meal a bustard made, for with flocks of hundreds of these primarily ground-dwelling birds strolling across the landscape there was a plentiful supply of these meaty creatures that were known as 'Plains Turkeys'. Populations of bustards came under sustained attack as settlers colonised new areas, hunted the birds for food and introduced sheep and cattle to the grasslands that the birds had ruled since the Dreamtime. Although they survived the onslaught, these large and distinctive birds now exist in greatly reduced numbers.

Today bustards are usually seen alone, with a mate or in a small group rather than in the extensive flocks that were once a common sight and at Culgoa Floodplain National Park, in south-western Queensland, I encountered a solitary bird that was doing what bustards have done for millennia. In the haughty pose that's characteristic of its species, with its long neck erect and its head sloping backwards, it was striding slowly through the tall grasses of the outback plains. The moment it became aware of my presence it glared in my direction with a distinctive and arrogant expression that I interpreted, quite accurately I'm sure, as something rather rude but that in polite terminology might be translated as "Please go away and leave me in peace."

"Don't worry! You're not on the menu now," I replied in little more than a whisper, "so just ignore

me and consider me to be as inconspicuous and harmless as a solitary ant swimming through a vat of treacle." Apparently convinced that I posed no threat, the bird continued its daily routine of searching for the wide range of foods that would satisfy its appetite and that include grasshoppers and other insects, small reptiles, rodents and frogs, with foliage, fruit and seeds scoffed as the second course.

Further north, in the remote Diamantina National Park, I encountered a small flock of bustards. I'd never dare to claim that these birds are lazy although sometimes it seems to be the case, but the reality is that they invariably take life easy and prefer to walk rather than fly. As soon as they realised that they'd been spotted they strode confidently into a maze of dense grasses and low vegetation and, when they considered that they'd put enough distance between themselves and me, they echoed the survival tactics that are employed by every other

member of their species. They simply stood still in the belief that by remaining motionless they had donned a cloak of invisibility and with the natural camouflage offered by their mottled brown plumage they were almost correct in that assumption.

When their primary tactic in their effort to elude danger failed and as I continued to creep stealthily towards them, they took no dramatic action to escape my unwanted attention but simply turned their backs on me and dawdled on their way as though harnessing a belief in their own invincibility. Every now and then they stopped briefly and turned their heads to assess the situation with their facial expressions hinting that they had little concern about the situation. "I'm no threat at all," I murmured discreetly but it wasn't my presence that suddenly drew their attention.

Bustards are among Australia's largest birds and are stocky characters that look as though they were never designed for flight but it's an option that they utilise as the last resort when danger comes too close and all other strategies have failed. As a Red Kangaroo came bounding across the plains in their direction the birds spread their wings and headed to the skies with unexpected agility.

They occasionally fly up into a tree to roost at night but on the plains that are their primary habitat, and where trees are as rare as a teenager without a mobile phone, bustards have no option other than to sleep on the ground and they lay their eggs on the bare soil or on a patch of grass. The eggs and vulnerable chicks provide easy pickings for predators, including foxes, feral cats and Dingoes but these great birds of the plains, which continue to take the twists and turns of fate in their stride, do little more than sit quietly with their young and hope that Mother Nature will do her utmost to ensure the survival of their species.

Where you'll find them: Bustards can be found grasslands and open woodlands in inland and northern areas of mainland Australia.

Emu

Dromaius novaehollandiae

My first encounter with an Emu was many years ago when I worked at a wildlife sanctuary and was tasked with relocating a bird that had become aggressive towards visitors. Getting an Emu to cooperate is about as easy as capturing a swarm of mosquitos in a colander and with the bird having to be moved from a picnic area to an enclosure that was a considerable distance away the only idea that I and my colleagues could conjure up was to trap it against a fence, tie its legs together and transport it in a wheelbarrow. That was when things became not only hazardous but also incredibly hilarious, although the Emu didn't seem to find the occasion any more entertaining than an all night game of tiddlywinks with a dodo.

The Emu, with a height of around 2 metres, is the largest bird in Australia and the second largest in the world after the African Ostrich. It features prominently on the Australian coat of arms. Despite its iconic status it's often regarded as a comical character and it only has itself to blame, for it's frequently encountered in some hilarious situations.

I first met a truly wild Emu on the golf course at the Queensland outback town of Yowah where, on greens that consisted of nothing more than sand, it was eating abandoned golf balls. When locals threateningly waved their golf clubs in the bird's direction it returned their angry shouts with a haughty stare that silently said, "You don't really think you scare me, do you?" and it arrogantly sauntered off to see what other delectable treasures it could find.

I've seen flocks of hundreds of Emus on the vast plains of the outback but it was in the sleepy Queensland town of Bollon, where a small group dawdled nonchalantly along the main road, that I asked the perennial question "Why did the chicken – or in this case the Emu – cross the road?" The answer was blatantly obvious as, thumbing their noses at growling trucks and massive road trains, the mob headed across the highway, from the parkland on one side to a house on the other and wandered in through an open gate to feed on the lawn before settling down to doze beneath the foliage of a shading tree.

A mob of Emus were just as blasé about the traffic on another rural road and I chuckled with laughter as my vehicle was forced to a standstill by a bird that was bathed in a large puddle in the Flinders Ranges in northern South Australia. It was thrashing its great wings around, sending water spraying high into the air and as it replicated the cleaning ritual of the far smaller birds that routinely utilise my garden bird bath, I was doubled up with laughter.

The Emu is unable to fly but it's certainly no slow poke for it can run at speeds of 40km/h or more and, near the Queensland outback town of Quilpie, a flock of Emus that had been quietly feeding beside the road irrationally opted for a change of pace. As they raced beside my campervan one bird glared in through the window as if to say "I bet we can beat you if we really try," but others had a different idea and turned abruptly across the road, brushing the front of my vehicle with their billowing skirts of feathers before, in a demonstration of their usual indecisive action, they turned abruptly once again and rushed back the way they'd come.

Another entertaining encounter of the Emu kind occurred at Currawinya National Park in south-western Queensland when I was woken, at dawn, by the mournful howl of a Dingo. I cautiously stepped from my campervan to be greeted not by any savage carnivore but by pelicans that were patrolling the perpetually muddy waters of the Paroo River that was at my doorstep, by White-plumed Honeyeaters that were dining on the flowers of riverbank Yapunyah trees, and by a family of Red Kangaroos that were quietly grazing on golden grasses that glinted with dew drops as the first rays of the sun crept across the horizon. "Good morning all," I murmured jovially as I set out for a brief pre-breakfast walk through the surrounding woodlands and I didn't have far to go before I encountered more imposing members of the outback's wildlife community.

A male Emu was striding towards me, wearing an expression that was one of displeasure rather than of welcoming acceptance of my presence and it was easy to see why he appeared so grumpy. I was standing between him and the river, which was where he and his gaggle of chicks were heading. "I'm no threat to you and those little blokes in their striped and fluffy pyjamas," I said but as old man Emu emitted loud grunts of aggression and became increasingly agitated I took the hint and made a hasty retreat. He nodded his head as though acknowledging my consideration and nudged his reluctant chicks towards the water where they nervously dabbled their toes in the mud and sipped at the murky soup of the Paroo.

Male Emus are dedicated and highly protective parents, unlike the females of the species that dutifully lay their eggs in a primitive nest on the ground then do a bunk and leave their mate to incubate the eggs and raise the chicks alone. Despite increasing hunger and thirst old man Emu stubbornly refuses to leave the eggs unattended for even a nanosecond and survives without either food or water for the entire eight weeks that it takes for the eggs to hatch. By then he's little more than an emaciated bundle of feathers and, having lost a third of his body weight, he looks as miserable as a wasp that thought it had flown into a jar of jam but found itself stomping through a pot of glue.

Every doting father Emu is a harsh disciplinarian and it was easy to see that the chicks had already learnt that they have to do exactly as they're told, primarily for their own safety. As a small flock of their relatives approached the little family that were loitering at the water's edge, old man Emu, with sounds that his chicks immediately understood and that alerted them to the possibility of danger, turned and walked briskly away, with the young birds obediently following in his footsteps.

Emus are perfectly designed for survival in harsh conditions. They feed on the tough and fibrous leaves of grasses and a wide range of native plants in addition to small fruits, flowers and insects, with a few stones, or golf balls, ingested to assist in the digestive process. They have translucent secondary eyelids that slide horizontally across their eyes to provide protection from dust and large claws on their massive feet that provide the weapons they require to fight other birds that invade their territory or threaten their chicks. As other birds wandered towards his vulnerable offspring, father Emu demonstrated his paternal skills. With his head lowered he charged towards the interlopers and leapt at the closest bird with his powerful feet and claws thrust forward. In that terrifying moment of aggression every wild creature was reminded not to tangle with old man Emu or to offer even a veiled hint of a threat towards his chicks.

Where you'll find them: Emus are most prominent in arid and semi-arid inland regions, but can also be found in lesser numbers in coastal and hinterland areas, with some occasionally seen on beaches and golf courses and in agricultural areas. The birds occasionally venture into urban areas when severe droughts deplete their familiar sources of food and water.

Laughing Kookaburra

Dacelo novaeguineae

I've met kookaburras on more occasions than there are toes on a thousand centipedes and I've listened to them, day after day, waking the world at dawn with their inimitable cackling laughter – they are also known as the Laughing Jackass – but despite their familiarity I have few complaints when one of these iconic birds once again demands my attention.

They often appear to be as lethargic as comatose barnacles but kookaburras, although they're frequently seen sitting quietly and motionlessly on a weathered stump or a fence post, are definitely not couch potatoes. They're simply birds with an abundance of patience and rather than expend their energy hunting for prey they prefer to wait for a meal to come to them.

These iconic birds feast primarily on insects, reptiles and frogs and, as members of the kingfisher family, fish is occasionally on their menu too. I've watched a bird dive into a pond in my garden

and emerge with a struggling goldfish in its bill and on such occasions I complain vociferously. "Why do you have to steal my fish when there are plenty of grasshoppers, caterpillars and other pests that I'd be pleased to see the back of?" I shouted in frustration as a kookaburra landed on a branch above the pond and tucked into its feast, but the only response I received to my angry outburst was an arrogant stare that I could only interpret as meaning, "I'll eat whatever I like and if you think you can stop me, then you'd better think again mate!"

I was less concerned about a bird's dining options when, one summer afternoon, I spotted a kookaburra on what passes for a lawn in my garden. It had a worm in its great bill, or at least the beginning of a worm and I was enthralled by the unique spectacle of bird and worm engaged in a life-and-death tug of war for this was no ordinary worm. It was a metre-long Giant Earthworm. "There's no way you can possibly eat all of it," I said as the bird continued to strain to pull the worm from the ground and crammed it, inch by inch, into its bill and bulging throat. To prove me wrong, it finally extracted the entire worm and ate and ate and ate until every morsel was gone.

Kookaburras are dedicated scroungers that frequently visit picnic and forested camping areas where they know there'll always be a free lunch. My encounters with birds in such places have not always been pleasurable however and on one occasion an arrogant little so-and-so zoomed down from its perch in a nearby tree and attempted to snatch a sandwich from my hand. I swung my hand at the bird, but with dazzlingly quick reactions it attacked again and, with a clatter of its large bill, ripped a lump of bread from my sandwich. It carried its prize to a lofty perch where it peered down at me as it dined on its takeaway meal. The expression on its face allowed me to read its mind and the message I received was "I'll be back for more when I've finished this bit."

When the flames of a campfire or of a raging bushfire hint that roasted snacks may be on offer kookaburras are one of the first birds on the scene. They wait patiently until the flames have

subsided or keep a beady eye out for insects, small reptiles, rodents or other creatures that have escaped the inferno only to find that Death has arrived with its wings flapping and its bill snapping.

Danger, for kookaburras, comes in varied guises and for a bird at the forested Barrington Tops National Park in New South Wales the threat was initiated by campers who had left a fire pit littered with broken bottles. The practiced scrounger, rummaging through the ashes for any hint of food, grasped the neck of a bottle and reached beyond its jagged edges to see if it contained anything edible. "Don't touch it! Don't touch it!" I shouted as I rushed towards the bird and, startled by my outburst, it dropped the bottle and fled, uninjured, from the scene. As I carefully removed every fragment of glass I cursed those stupid and inconsiderate members of the human race who had given no thought to the possible consequences of their foolish actions.

The kookaburras that are regular visitors to my forested garden face none of the dangers often put in their path by humans and when they're looking for a home in which to start a new family they have no trouble in finding suitable accommodation in the vicinity. They often utilise a vacant hollow in an old tree but have no reluctance about sharing their accommodation with other wild creatures and I watched a pair laboriously, peck by peck, excavate a hole in an arboreal termite's nest. Several weeks later, having kept an eye on the birds' continual comings and goings, I clambered cautiously up a ladder to peer into the nest and was met by the startled gaze of a newly hatched chick that, being little more than an ungainly pink blob dominated by a gigantic bill, was as attractive as a swarm of maggots in a wet paper bag. Ultimately, like a Cinderella of the avian world, it became a true beauty as it donned its gown of mottled brown plumage but it looked far from happy with its first experience of the world. Within minutes of leaving the relative comfort of its nest the landscape was subjected to a deluge of biblical proportions and the bedraggled bird soon looked as miserable as a frog in a cavern of vipers.

Another chick from another nest experienced a rough start to its life too when, perhaps too curious for its own good, it tumbled from its nest. I found it lying on the road that slices through the forest near my home. With its nest too high to reach I had no option other than to adopt it myself but I wasn't alone in my attempts to care for the frail and naked creature.

It was kept in a warm indoor environment every night and each morning I carried it outside to a large enclosure where it would be safe from predators. I fed it with fat and juicy grubs that I dug up from the compost heap but I wasn't the only one providing a continual supply of food. The local family of kookaburras demonstrated their ability to work together and, heeding the chick's subtle yet constant calls, they provided it with a succession of snacks, coming and going all day long to satisfy its seemingly insatiable appetite while others kept watch for danger from their perches on nearby fence posts and trees.

The youngster grew rapidly and one day, as I was carrying it on my arm from the shed to the enclosure, it made its first attempt to fly, an attempt that saw it nose dive to the ground as quickly as a raft made from lead would sink in a flooded stream. "You'll have to practise a bit more before you try that again," I advised the stunned bird that took my suggestion and spent much of the day stretching its wings and jumping up and down, much to the delight of the audience of its relatives.

The following day it tried again and as it made its first flight it seemed to be beaming with joy, joy that rivalled my pleasure at its survival, although my happiness was tinged with sadness at its departure from my life. "Perhaps you'll come back again soon," I called as the fledgling, accompanied by its extended family, vanished among the trees to hopefully live happily ever after. It was, for another bird, a story with a very happy ending.

Where you'll find them: Laughing Kookaburras can be found in woodlands and open forests throughout eastern Australia. They were introduced to both Tasmania and Western Australia, where they pose a threat to the survival of some native species.

Sacred Kingfisher

Todiramphus sanctus

Polynesian islanders once revered the Sacred Kingfisher as a being that could miraculously control the ocean's waves and calm its raging tantrums. It's one of the most commonly seen of the 10 species of kingfishers that call Australia home and although I've seen this glamorous bird beside rivers and lakes and darting through the darkest of forests I've never seen it within cooee of the sea.

It was on a leisurely kayaking journey along the Paroo River in outback Queensland that I first encountered one of these dazzling birds. All I saw in that memorable moment was a vivid flash of blue that streaked through the darkness of the riverbank woodlands, but since then I've seen the Sacred Kingfisher in all its glory on many occasions. I've watched it dive from a branch, a power cable or other lofty vantage point and silently snatch a small lizard, a frog or an insect from the ground and return to its perch to enthusiastically scoff its prey. I've seen Sacred Kingfishers

in my forested garden too and I'm always relieved that the bird's common name is somewhat misleading, for although they have the necessary skills, these colourful kingfishers have little interest in catching aquatic prey. They occasionally take advantage of the fish that, with their vivid orange colouring, are as conspicuous in the dark water of the garden's ponds as a wake of vultures in a deserted desert graveyard but most times when they splash down into the water from an overhanging branch that they routinely use as their personal diving board it's only for a bath and the fish are ignored. Fortunately they prefer a wide range of terrestrial prey and settle for an aquatic snack only when other

food is in short supply and during the breeding season when they have hungry chicks to satisfy.

When the breeding season approaches Sacred Kingfishers demonstrate that they're certainly not afraid of hard yakka and they begin the arduous task of creating a safe and secure home for their new family. Sometimes they utilise a hollow in a tree as a readymade home but a termite nest on the trunk of a tree that's close to water forms the basis of their preferred accommodation and I've often watched birds tenaciously utilising their bills as jack hammers to sculpt the hard 'soil' of a termites' nest and to excavate a large hole in which to create their own cosy nest. The termites quickly repair the damage and seal their living quarters off from those of the squatters and both birds and insects settle down to live side by side as the most tolerant of neighbours.

I have as much chance of seeing what's going on in a Sacred Kingfisher's nest as I have of seeing a fish knitting a pair of socks but I always know when the chicks have hatched and as their muted calls emanate from the nest I smile with pleasure and satisfaction in the knowledge that new life has arrived in the bush. This is a time when death is never far away either, for with ravenous and continually nagging chicks to feed fish is invariably on the Sacred Kingfisher's shopping list. "I'm sure you won't take any more than you really need but please put them out of their misery as quickly as possible," I've muttered a hundred times or more when my goldfish have come under sustained attack but when I receive the kingfisher's momentary glare that I can only interpret as meaning "So stop me if you can!" I know I'm wasting my breath and that I must become resigned

to the inevitable and hard facts of life and accept the reality that the death of a few fish is the price I must pay for the honour of sharing my forest environment with these beautiful birds.

Fortunately, Sacred Kingfishers never arrive in marauding hordes for these are birds that are dedicated loners and that have no interest in others of their species until they feel the urge to start a family and that's something for which I'm always grateful.

Where you'll find them: These kingfishers are found in all coastal regions of Australia, with their primary habitat being woodlands and forests that hem coastal estuaries and tidal inlets, or that are close to streams, rivers and wetlands.

Australian Brush-turkey

Alectura lathami

"What was that?" I shouted in excitement as, while driving along a forest-hemmed track in south-eastern Queensland, a large dark creature rushed across my path from one shaded retreat to another. But as soon as the words had left my mouth I realised that the black bird that had been in such a frantic hurry could be nothing other than a brush-turkey.

Also known as scrub-turkeys. Australian Brush-turkeys are the largest of Australia's three megapodes, a trio of primarily terrestrial birds that includes the Orange-footed Scrubfowl and the Malleefowl. All three build large nesting mounds. The only one of the group that most people will ever see is the brush-turkey, for this is a species that's as common in its extensive range as blowflies around a decaying desert carcass. I've often seen them scurrying through forests and woodlands but unfortunately it's other encounters, those of the close and personal kind, that have left me fuming with frustration and that have been the most memorable events for all the wrong reasons.

When camping in a forest that spilled down to the ocean at Inskip Point, near the Queensland town of Rainbow Beach, one of the arrogant little so-and-sos invaded my territory and as I shooed it away, knowing that it would be up to no good, it glowered at me with what could only be described as a dirty look. "I'm just doing what comes naturally and I'm allowed to look for food aren't I?" the bird seemed to ask with an undisguised air of arrogance, but the food it had its eye on was mine. Ignoring my efforts to evict it from what I had temporarily claimed as my personal

domain it vigorously scratched among the forest's carpet of leaf litter and hurled the sand that it exposed in every direction, including into the stew that was simmering on the stove and over the camera that I'd left on a chair, and while I was distracted by the antics of one bird its mates hopped onto the table to help themselves to my food as others ransacked my tent in search of any tasty and unguarded treats.

The stew had been rendered inedible and sand-clogged dials made the camera completely inoperable. As I chased the birds away with shouts of uncharacteristic anger I'm sure I glimpsed smiles of satisfaction on the faces of the vandals as they ran to the beach. As they strolled across the sand, each bird bearing the arrogant look of an innocent falsely accused of a crime, they pecked at the fallen fruits of the native fig trees that lined the shore and the ring leader gave its mates a brief glance that enquired, "What is that human so upset about? All we were doing was looking for food!"

Brush-turkeys have become accustomed to the presence of humans and have minimal fear of the planet's dominant species. I love to see them in their wild environment when they're doing nothing more damaging than rummaging for a feast of insects and worms followed by a second course of fruit and seeds, but when they arrive in my garden, a place that they seem to regard as an inviting extension of their natural habitat, I'm as happy as a bee that thinks it's found a flower and stumbles into the gaping mouth of a Venus Flytrap.

I've got no complaints when a solitary bird dawdles across a garden bed, knowing that it will be providing some assistance in controlling insect pests, but it was a different story one winter's day when a male arrived on the scene with the sole intention of building a nesting mound. He rampaged through the garden as though it was his personal kingdom, a place in which he could do as he liked with no regard for the consequences of his actions, for his only aim was to ultimately increase the population of his species. He tenaciously scratched up fallen leaves, small plants, bulbs and mulch leaving the ground bare, with the destruction bringing tears to my eyes. Every attempt to deter him from his task seemed doomed to failure and day after day he continued to wreak havoc across the garden. "With acres of forest right on the doorstep, why must you build your mound right here?" I demanded as, with waving arms and screams of anger, I repetitively chased him away from my most valued plants.

Brush-turkeys fly only to escape from danger and to roost in trees, and all the villain of this story did was to flutter away to what both he and I regarded as a safe distance. But as soon as my back was turned, when I'd silently boasted to myself that I had won the battle though not the war, Mister Persistence himself returned to continue his task. It's a game we play year after year – I chase and shout, he runs and hides. I rub my hands with a moment of satisfaction at my brief victory and as he leaves the scene of destruction I rake every skerrick of mulch back to where it should be, but the moment I've lowered my guard he returns and drags half of my garden to his ever-growing mound once again to create a nest that's now some 4 metres in diameter and a metre high.

I'd be charged with obscenity if I dared to write the words I've uttered with more than a hint of rage when a brush-turkey has redesigned my garden. Fortunately I'm offered a brief respite when he's ready to look for several mates who will all obligingly lay their eggs in his heap of debris. The females, having no maternal instincts, simply do what's expected of them and then walk away and abandon their eggs. The decomposing vegetation of the mound generates the heat that's required for the incubation of the eggs and the fastidious male bird, utilising a highly sensitive area near his bill, continually tests the temperature of the mound and adds or removes material as required.

The horde of chicks that eventually hatch have the arduous task of digging their way out of the nesting mound and each emerges fully dressed in a cloak of dark brown feathers. From day one the little birds are on their own with no one other than Mother Nature to guide them along life's bumpy road, but with the inherited knowledge of what constitutes a good meal and where to find it starvation is not among the many dangers that the vulnerable chicks face.

Recently, when I was enjoying lunch on the patio, I could hardly believed my eyes when a tiny brush-turkey confidently strode across the floor and although I'm always pleased to see new life emerge I couldn't disguise my displeasure. "You're as welcome here as a shoal of piranhas in a goldfish pond and I'd be pleased if you'd scarper," I grumbled to the baby bird that, only a few days earlier, had been little more than the yolk of an egg. "I won't deny that you certainly look adorable but unfortunately you're genetically programmed to be a genuine pain in the backside."

"Me! A pain in the backside!" the chick's arrogant glare seemed to say as it froze in its tracks the moment it saw me. Its icy stare of disdain aimed its message in my direction. "I'm here now and I'm not going anywhere in a hurry" and, demonstrating the arrogance of the adults of its

species, it strolled into the garden and, tossing fallen leaves and mulch in every direction, it scratched beneath a congestion of shrubs for the insects that it instinctively knew would provide the sustenance it would need to survive. I admired its youthful tenacity and its ability to be fully independent at a time in life when the fledglings of other species were vociferously demanding to be fed by their doting parents, but I live in hope that every new generation of brush-turkeys will eventually move on to new and distant territories. I enjoy each encounter with these imposing birds when they're in their natural environment but I pray that these bold and confident creatures never again set foot in my garden.

Where you'll find them: Brush-turkeys inhabit an extensive region on the eastern side of the continent that stretches from the Cape York Peninsula in northern Queensland to central New South Wales. Although they typically inhabit damp forests and woodlands, they can also be seen in other bushland environments and in urban areas.

Squatter Pigeon
Geophaps scripta

Squatter Pigeons once strode and fluttered across the western plains of New South Wales but life hasn't been kind to these relatively small birds and today, in this section of their range, they're teetering on the verge of extinction and are listed as an endangered species. That means that the chance of spotting one of these distinctive birds in the most southerly extremity of their range is on a par with the possibility that a deep sea diver might glimpse a fish knitting a pair of socks, but fortunately the Squatter Pigeon is still alive and well in the more northerly parts of the continent.

There's no glitz and glamour about Squatter Pigeons, for Mother Nature has dressed them in primarily brown and white attire but she certainly knew what she was doing. These are predominantly ground-dwelling birds and it's the highly effective camouflage provided by their

relatively drab plumage that has enabled them to survive, despite the dangers they continually face. The impact of land clearing on their habitat, the reduction in the availability of food as a result of droughts and overgrazing by livestock, and predation by feral cats and foxes continue to have a dramatic impact on populations of these pigeons with their numbers having declined in the northern areas of their range to such an extent that they're now listed, in this area, as a vulnerable species.

My first glimpse of this attractive bird was near the central Queensland town of Calliope when, during a leisurely journey from one rural destination to another, I stopped to photograph the forested landscape and there it was, a solitary Squatter Pigeon, pretending that it was invisible among the mayhem of fallen branches that had been tossed to the ground by a recent storm.

"Someone once said that life wasn't meant to be easy and that's certainly true for you and your mates," I whispered as I tiptoed cautiously towards the little bird. It stared at me with a quizzical expression that queried what this unfamiliar creature that had the temerity to intrude into its domain might be. I stood as quietly and motionlessly as a marble angel in a deserted desert graveyard but the Squatter Pigeon, one of the most timid of birds, was taking no chances and, with a silent flutter of its wings, it vanished from sight in less time than it takes for a spider to blink all eight of its beady little eyes.

That, I assumed, was the last I'd ever see of Squatter Pigeons, until one pleasant autumn morning when I was heading on a new adventure to explore the remote Goodedulla National Park that lies to the west of the central Queensland city of Rockhampton. As my campervan

bumped along a rugged and meandering track the pangs of hunger urged me to stop for a cuppa and a bite to eat and a grassy clearing beside a small dam provided the perfect spot for a break. While I impatiently waited for the billy to boil, swathes of tall golden grasses nodded in the gentlest of breezes like a chattering throng of hardworking scarecrows. A pair of Australian Wood Ducks drifted silently on the dam's calm blue water and Sulphur-crested Cockatoos, startled by my arrival, abandoned their perch on a rickety wooden gate and fled into the azure sky. As I looked at every feature of the surrounding forest I saw something that was almost as unexpected as the sight of a chameleon rowing across the Pacific Ocean in a colander. I saw a small flock of Squatter Pigeons. They were feeding on the ground, as these elusive little birds usually do and were foraging for seeds that, along with the occasional insect or two that are tossed in for good measure, are the staple ingredients of their diet.

"Fancy seeing you elusive little fellas here," I whispered as I slowly inched closer and closer to the birds that appeared completely unaware or unconcerned by my presence. One began to shuffle across the track and looked back at its companions as if to say, "Are you lot coming or what?" and as they heeded their mate's request and trotted across the road with a comical gait they glanced back momentarily in my direction before disappearing from sight as rapidly as an ice cube on a bonfire.

Where you'll find them: In central and north-eastern Queensland, where they inhabit open woodlands that have an understorey of grass and that are close to a reliable source of water.

Superb Lyrebird

Menura novaehollandiae

Once under threat as a result of the widespread destruction of their habitat, populations of Superb Lyrebirds have bounced back and today they're regarded as a relatively common species. That doesn't mean that they're easy to see however, for as birds with predominantly dark brown plumage which spend most of their time on the ground, they're well camouflaged among the shadows and low vegetation of the forests that they call home. They often give their presence away with an astounding array of calls, but many of their vocal sounds bear no resemblance to the chirps, twitters and squawks of other birds.

One cold and frosty winter's morning, as I wandered along a remote walking trail in the Barrington Tops National Park in New South Wales, I heard a car door slamming and an engine revving and was puzzled as to where any vehicle could possibly be. Then a black-cockatoo screeched, a whipbird's distinctive call reverberated through the forest and a dog barked and

suddenly I realised that what I was hearing was a Superb Lyrebird demonstrating the superb act of mimicry for which this species is justifiably famous.

These avian celebrities have the most sophisticated vocal skills of any member of the animal kingdom other than humans and although males are the most vociferous, females find plenty to sing about too. Superb Lyrebirds sing throughout the year but it's during the breeding season, from June to August, when their performance is at its best. They blend their own less than memorable song with an eclectic array of sounds that mimic not only the songs of other birds but also any other noise that has caught their attention. Their seemingly limitless repertoire may include the growl of a Koala, the howl of a Dingo and less natural noises such as that of a chainsaw, a fire alarm, rifle shots, the click of a camera's shutter or the ringtone of a mobile phone.

Some 80 per cent of the Superb Lyrebird's songs imitate the calls of other birds and they're mimicked so accurately that even the birds whose calls the lyrebirds use are fooled into responding to what they have erroneously assumed is the voice of one of their own species. That's incredible enough but the most amazing fact is that many of the calls of lyrebirds are sounds that they've learnt from their parents or have heard performed by other members of their community and they often sing the songs of birds that haven't shared their neck of the woods for many years.

When I was camping in the heart of the forests of the Wollemi National Park, near the New South Wales town of Kandos, it wasn't a vocal performance that alerted me to the presence of Superb Lyrebirds. The light rain of an icy winter's morning turned the golden flames of my campfire to tufts of smoke but the inclement weather failed to dampen my enthusiasm for wildlife

and I wandered off to see what wondrous creatures would be out and about. A faint sound momentarily disrupted the silence and I stood and waited for a repeat of the noise so I could home in on its origins. What I eventually found was a pair of Superb Lyrebirds and it was their incessant scratching as they foraged for food among the leaf litter strewn across the forest floor and outcrops of boulders that had revealed their presence. "This is my domain and I'll scratch up as many leaves as I want to," a bird seemed to say as it glared at me with a defiant expression. "Then just get on with it mate," I replied quietly. "I've got no intention of interrupting your efforts." As I stood silently, attempting to blend into the landscape, the birds continued to search for their favoured foods, which include caterpillars, centipedes, spiders and earthworms. The male waved his large and ornate tail as though taunting me to move and take his photo but I steadfastly remained motionless as I watched the birds' activities from the forest's icy shadows.

Superb Lyrebirds can fly but rarely do so unless sheer terror persuades them to flutter to a place that's beyond any danger. As I eventually shuffled from one frozen foot to another the birds turned and scurried away, their highly decorative tails offering the avian equivalent of a two-finger salute as they vanished among the rocks and shadows of the enveloping vegetation.

Where you'll find them: Superb Lyrebirds inhabit damp forests and rainforests in south-eastern Australia, with their range stretching from southern Victoria to south-eastern Queensland. They are also found in southern Tasmania.

Tawny Frogmouth

Podargus strigoides

The Tawny Frogmouth is a bird that's not renowned for being noisy and demonstrative. It usually keeps a very low profile, and on the occasions when I've encountered this curious character it's only been my keen eyesight that has revealed its presence. It's a nocturnal species and with its mottled brown plumage and its habit of spending its days perching on a branch with its eyes closed and its head pointing upwards in such a way that it looks like part of nature's furniture, it usually resembles just another piece of old and weathered wood,

One day, as I walked through the forests of the New England National Park near the New South Wales town of Armidale, I was admiring the varied vegetation and it was only with a good slice of luck that I happened to spot a Tawny Frogmouth. She had a very good reason for remaining even quieter and even more discreet than members of this species would usually be during daylight hours, for she was sitting on her nest waiting patiently for her eggs to hatch. "You've got a good

excuse for taking life as easy as a geriatric centipede," I whispered as she peered down from her lofty abode with an expression of boredom, "and good luck with your new family."

Later, in the ranges that surround the New South Wales town of Dorrigo, I'd stopped beside an isolated cottage to ask for directions to my next destination but was distracted by a subtle noise that eventually lured me into the darkness of the surrounding forest. There, beside the trunk of a lofty Eucalyptus tree, a Tawny Frogmouth sat huddled beside its mate, with its gentle, repetitive, almost purring sound being all that had given its presence away. "Mother Nature gave you the perfect plumage for camouflage but you've been spotted mate," I murmured as the birds stared, with large unblinking eyes, in my direction. "Don't worry. I won't come any closer and you can head back to the land of nod," I added as I retreated from the scene.

Tawny Frogmouths are often referred to as 'owls' but they are unrelated to any owl. In common with owls, they have the large eyes and excellent hearing that are required to be efficient nocturnal predators but their feet, which lack the curved talons of owls, are not used for capturing and tearing apart some hapless victim.

During daylight hours they're almost as lethargic as a slab of frozen lasagne and even during the night they often demonstrate little enthusiasm for energetic activities and employ the simplest of techniques to obtain a meal. They dawdle silently along the ground and pounce on their prey, which include insects, rodents, small lizards, frogs, worms, slugs and snails – and it doesn't require much more than the speed and agility of a comatose tortoise to grab some of these slow-moving creatures.

Tawny Frogmouths, in their most energetic of moods, will swoop from a lofty perch to snatch moths and other flying insects from the air and it was during such a moment of hunting that I had another memorable avian encounter. As I was driving along a country road at night a bird swooped through the air to catch a small creature illuminated by the headlights. Despite braking hard, my vehicle collided with the bird. I found it standing at the side of the road and picked it up, assuming that it was injured, and it sat on my hand, gazing into my eyes with its golden eyes as though asking "What happened? I just leapt off my perch to grab a takeaway meal and I can't remember a thing after that!"

"Let's see what the damage is mate. I'm sure you'll be okay and on your way again very soon" I whispered optimistically as I examined the frogmouth for any obvious injuries but I found none. It sat perfectly still, its eyes following every slow and calculated movement of my bird-free hand, its scaly feet and long claws holding my fingers in a vice-like grip. I tried to toss the bird into the air, hoping that it was well enough to fly into the darkness but it merely steadied itself by extending its wings and grasping my hand even tighter and stared at me as if to say "Please let me sit here a little longer!"

Many years ago an old man told me that when a bird was stunned following a collision with a window or a vehicle I should try whistling to it, and the bird seemed impressed by the first bars of my tune and began to look a little more alert. "I'm no great musician," I said in apology "but I'll whistle for a little longer if it makes you feel better." As each second passed the patient's demeanour appeared to improve, then suddenly, quite unexpectedly, it spread its wings and vanished into the black curtain of the night.

Tawny Frogmouths are monogamous birds that can live for up to 14 years. When a pair has found a habitat in which they're as happy as caterpillars in a tossed salad they spend their entire lives there, but when forests are felled by loggers or when bulldozers clear land for houses or agriculture the birds' world is destroyed as quickly as Peter Piper could pick a peck of pickled peppers. Land-clearing practices have resulted in a decline in many populations of these beautiful creatures in recent years and I tremble at the thought that future generations might never have the opportunity for a face-to-face encounter with these secretive and curious birds of the night.

Where you'll find them: Throughout Australia, including Tasmania, in a wide range of habitats, from forests and woodlands to urban and agricultural environments, but they draw the line at rainforests and treeless deserts.

HONEYEATERS

Noisy Friarbird

Philemon corniculatus

The Noisy Friarbird's species name is derived from the Latin word *'corniculum,'* meaning 'a little horn,' but rather than a horn, all this honeyeater carries on its bill is a conspicuous lump that's referred to as a casque. It's the bird's voice more than this distinctive feature of its anatomy that ensures that the Noisy Friarbird is always as conspicuous as a flock of butterflies gatecrashing a convention of glove puppets, for it's rarely quiet for more than a second or two and that means that its presence in any forest or woodland environment is never a well-kept secret.

I've seen and heard Noisy Friarbirds in many locations from central Queensland to Victoria, and as they're permanent residents of my garden and the surrounding forests I encounter these hyperactive chatterboxes every day of the year.

Noisy by name and noisy by nature, they communicate with others of their kind with an astounding array of calls that might replicate the garbled conversation of a horde of inebriated vampires. Their message could never be interpreted as something as courteous as "How are you today, mate?" for Noisy Friarbirds are rather antisocial where other species are concerned and even those of their own kind that have the temerity to invade their domain and that expect to feast on any flowers that one of these large and bossy honeyeaters has claimed as its own won't receive a warm welcome.

They routinely visit flowering Grevilleas and Callistemons and the entertaining acrobatic performances of Noisy Friarbirds, as they gorge themselves on the nectar-laden blooms, are dominated by demonstrations of agility and determination as the birds attain contorted poses and

often hang upside-down to reach the flowers at the tips of slender stems that bow beneath each bird's meagre weight.

In my garden it's the lofty Black Bean Tree (*Castanospermum australe*) that's their ultimate prize and a single bird stakes its claim to the tree's abundance of flowers with a complex medley of unique sounds, with the inimitable squawks and chirps of a rambling avian monologue that, in essence, says, "This is *my* tree." With his verbal message enhanced with a hefty serving of aggression the little dictator chases away every bird that dares to come too close, that has the temerity to set foot in the tree, or that flutters among the foliage of adjacent plants. "I'm sure there's enough nectar for others to share," I call out to the bird as it viciously defends its domain from any birds other than its own offspring but my words go unheeded, for when it comes to food, sharing nature's bounty is usually the last thing on the mind of any Noisy Friarbird.

Their varied diet, in addition to fruit and nectar, includes insects and they're particularly partial to a feast of grasshoppers – a fact which guarantees that I'm happy to overlook their aggressive ways and welcome them as invaluable allies in the ongoing battle to control insect pests in my extensive organic garden.

I always know when Noisy Friarbirds are feeling a little amorous and are intent on starting a family, for it's then that they tear long strips of bark from the trunks of ragged Melaleuca trees. It's a material that, together with strands of sticky cobweb, they utilise to construct their nests. When they've laid their eggs and are devotedly tending to the needs of their chicks tranquillity finally descends over the landscape as, for a brief period of time, Noisy Friarbirds have very little to say.

Where you'll find them: They thrive in a wide range of habitats that include eucalypt woodlands and forests that hem wetlands and waterways from coastal regions to arid and semi-arid areas of the continent. Their extensive range stretches from north-eastern Queensland to north-eastern Victoria, but when winter arrives in the southern extremity of their range the birds head north and only return south as warmer weather makes a welcome return.

Spiny-cheeked Honeyeater

Acanthagenys rufogularis

I've often heard the subtle song of the Spiny-cheeked Honeyeater, yet the bird has remained discreetly hidden from sight, for with its predominantly cream and brown speckled plumage it is often inconspicuous among the foliage of its woodland habitat.

My first encounter with this species was in Currawinya National Park in outback Queensland and all that initially captured my attention as I sat beside a campfire one winter's morning was the

bird's gently twittering voice. For a moment I silently debated what to do. Should I stay beside the fire, keep warm and remain unaware of who the owner of that cheerful song might be, or should I abandon any hint of comfort and face the prospect of shivering in the biting cold breeze as I attempted to satisfy my curiosity. Needless to say, the latter option won and after adding a thick scarf and warm gloves to my already thick bundle of clothing I wandered off into the woodlands that hem the Paroo River that is a vital artery that brings life to Currawinya.

I prowled stealthily among the trees, my footsteps on dry leaves and grasses frequently obliterating any hint of the bird's cacophony of curious sounds and whistling noises. I turned this way and that, trying to locate the direction from which the calls emanated, I peered into every cluster of vegetation, scanning every branch and finally spotted my quarry. It was instantly recognisable, thanks to its distinctive black-tipped pink bill, its blue eyes and the 'spiny' white cheek patches that have earned this shy, almost reclusive bird its common name.

"You're certainly an elusive character," I murmured as the bird was alerted to my arrival in its corner of the bush as I stumbled inelegantly over a log. "Please don't leave in too much of a hurry now that I've finally met you," I pleaded and it graciously conceded to my request and continued to whistle and twitter in its inimitable way.

Spiny-cheeked Honeyeaters are unlikely to ignore any flowers that offer copious amounts of nectar but if they have a choice they generally prefer fruit, with their preference being for the berries of mistletoe. They're continually on the move in search of the most delicious bush tucker but they never go hungry, for if fruit and flowers are temporarily unavailable they'll dine on insects that they often catch while in flight and, being unexpectedly savage little blighters, they'll prey on small lizards and will occasionally eat the tiny chicks of other birds.

Such a varied diet has enabled Spiny-cheeked Honeyeaters to thrive in a great diversity of habitats and in the early hours of a chilly winter morning, that time when night has retreated yet daylight has not yet arrived, I was meandering through the woodlands that line the shores of Lake Nuga Nuga, in central Queensland's Arcadia Valley and who should I meet other than a Spiny-cheeked Honeyeater. With its feathers fluffed up to make it appear to be twice its normal size the shivering bird looked as happy as a frog in a cavern of vipers, its face sculpted with an expression that allowed me to read its mind, an expression that clearly said "What am I doing in this miserable climate when I could have flown north?"

"Life can only get better mate," I whispered optimistically and right on cue the sun winked through the ragged clouds that were all that remained of the doona of night. The honeyeater looked up from its almost comatose state and, with a gaze that could only be interpreted as a smile, it began to sing its unique medley of calls. As the sun gradually chased away the cold hand of winter, life, for both bird and birdwatcher, met my prediction and only improved.

Where you'll find them: Spiny-cheeked Honeyeaters inhabit riverine woodlands and bushland dominated by mallee and Acacia scrub and carpeted by Spinifex grass. They can be found in many parts of the Australian mainland, although they're absent from northern tropical and eastern coastal regions and from the extreme south-eastern and south-western corners of the continent.

Singing Honeyeater

Lichenostomus virescens

I've never considered physical beauty to be the most important feature of any living creature and that's just as well, for the Singing Honeyeater, with its primarily grey and olive-brown plumage, certainly can't claim a prize for its good looks. As a bird that makes itself at home in a wide range of habitats, from coastal scrub to arid regions dominated by acacias, and rainforests with dense undergrowth, it's one of Australia's most widespread honeyeaters.

My first encounter with this species was an event that was almost as exciting as the thought of an evening with a wax effigy of Donald Trump, or even worse, an evening with the man himself. It seemed to be a shy and reclusive character and I was alerted to its fleeting presence only by its incessant melodious twittering. I caught barely a glimpse of this hyperactive honeyeater as it fluttered among the nectar-rich flowers of coastal shrubs in the Lincoln National Park on South Australia's Eyre Peninsula.

At Rainbow Valley, in the Northern Territory, I encountered a bird with a dramatically different personality to that of its southern relative – an extroverted little character rather than one drenched with timidity. After a long walk around the region's distinctive geological formations I returned to my campsite with the aim of doing nothing more than putting my feet up and relaxing with a cuppa and a bite to eat and hadn't expected any impromptu entertainment.

"You look as though you've got as much energy as a swarm of inebriated barnacles," my other half commented with his usual sarcasm when I slumped down into my chair in the shade of our campervan. "You're not wrong there," I replied. "So would you please do the honours and put the kettle on – and pass me a few grapes to eat while I wait?" "I'm at your service Ma'am," he dutifully replied with the respectful bow of the servant that he sometimes assumes he is and a bowl of grapes was in my hand in less time than it takes for a blowfly to dodge an imperfectly aimed fly swatter.

I gazed out at the late afternoon landscape where there was no sign of life, no whisper of even the most feeble of breezes among the low shrubs and grasses and no sign of any birds, but that changed abruptly when I carelessly dropped a solitary grape. A Singing Honeyeater miraculously appeared at my feet, pecked and stabbed frenetically at the fruit, then, having devoured the tasty snack, it stared up at me with a quizzical expression that demanded more. "Any bird that lives out here must know where to find natural bush tucker," I quietly scolded the bird, "So you shouldn't expect free handouts – and you certainly won't get any from me."

The Singing Honeyeater is certainly not the most glamorous of wild creatures but it's the bird's cheerful disposition that is its standout feature and it employed its most persuasive skills, twittering with its melodious voice, dancing around my feet and staring up at me with pleading eyes, in a performance that was almost enough to shatter my resolve to never feed wild birds.

Finally, resigned to the fact that nothing more was on offer, it returned to the dusty dregs of the grape, dragging it towards me as though hinting "more of this sweet stuff please." With no food forthcoming its cheerful pleading stare quickly turned to a scowl of anger and its muted twittering erupted into a voice of frustration as it flapped its wings wildly and rushed around my feet, jumping up and down in a frenetic temper tantrum.

"Don't move! Don't move!" I shouted in panic as my husband emerged from the campervan with the much-needed cuppa in his hand and took a step towards the ground. "We've been invaded by an army of one – and if you don't watch where you're going you'll either step on the little blighter or trip over it. There is such a thing as outstaying your welcome," I added, directing my words of frustration at the little bird as I tried to discourage its attentions with the poorly aimed flick of a tea towel, but my efforts were ignored by Mister Determination himself.

"There's only one way to keep both it and us out of harm's way," I mumbled with displeasure and I grudgingly tossed a grape into the distant grass. The bird, with the smile of victory on its face, fluttered off to capture its prize and scoffed it at a distance where we could watch its performance with no risk to either bird or human.

Singing Honeyeaters usually forage among shrubs and grasses for snacks of insects and sip on the nectar of flowers, but everyone is entitled to a special treat every now and then aren't they?

Where you'll find them: These honeyeaters occur west of the Great Dividing Range, in Queensland and New South Wales, in western Victoria and in most regions of South Australia. They are also widespread in Western Australia and the Northern Territory.

White-plumed Honeyeater

Ptilotula penicillatus

The White-plumed Honeyeater, being one of Australia's smallest honeyeaters, is an elusive little character that I've generally spotted more by luck that by any great powers of observation.

During one of the worst droughts in Australia's history I'd set up camp on the shaded banks of Nebine Creek, a diminutive yet vital waterway that slices through the Culgoa Floodplain National Park in outback Queensland. With all other sources of water in the region having been replaced by bowls of dust I was confident that hordes of thirsty creatures would flock to the area,

for the creek, although it was little more than a series of muddy pools, was all that would keep the Grim Reaper at bay. I settled down on a log close to the water's edge and waited impatiently as the curtain of dusk slowly descended over another beautiful yet dry day.

Red Kangaroos emerged from the surrounding bushland as Galahs and Red-rumped Parrots arrived to drink and from my front-row seat I silently applauded the continually changing cast of characters that paraded across this vast outdoor stage. I suppressed the urge to acknowledge every performer with wildly clapping hands and remained as quiet as a miser thumbing through the pile of banknotes under his mattress as White-plumed Honeyeaters eventually sauntered onto the stage. They fluttered down onto a fallen branch that was protruding from the stream and stretched down to drink, with their images reflected in the muddy water that was all that remained of the creek. The drought had arrived with Death as its companion and with the carcasses of kangaroos littering the landscape it was only raptors that had cause to celebrate Mother Nature's cruelty. "I'm praying that rain will come very soon, before the last pools of water evaporate," I whispered as the tiny birds, having quenched their thirst, flew into the trees and settled down for the night.

White-plumed Honeyeaters, which owe their common name to the streak of white feathers across each bird's neck, make themselves at home in the most remote of outback locations and it wasn't long after I'd set up camp in another corner of the Queensland outback that I met these attractive little honeyeaters once again.

It was the Paroo River that had lured not only me but also several species of birds to Currawinya National Park and with the Yapunyah trees (*Eucalyptus ochrophloia*) that line the river's banks draped with nectar-laden flowers, White-plumed Honeyeaters had made the right decision when choosing this beautiful spot as their feeding destination.

These are hyperactive little birds, birds that are always on the go and that never sit still for more than a fragment of a second. As they flitted from one tree to another and from one cluster of blooms to the next I felt almost as lethargic as an inebriated sloth in comparison to these energetic creatures that, with acrobatic antics and determination rivalling that of a fly swimming through a bowl of custard, attempted to reach the most unreachable of flowers.

Floral nectar is the favoured food of White-plumed Honeyeaters but they'll also scoff small fruits, eat insects that they snatch from the air while in flight and, being far from fastidious little critters, they'll also forage on the ground for seeds.

It was food that was uppermost on my mind when I drove into the Victorian town of Murtoa. I arrived at the local parklands with the intention of doing nothing more than having a picnic lunch, but as I sat down at a vacant table I realised that other diners were already feasting. Two White-plumed Honeyeaters, clambering among the yellow flowers of an adjacent eucalyptus tree, glared down at me with looks of utter disdain that I could only interpret as an avian message that in polite society would translate as "We didn't invite you to share our environment, so why don't you go away?" "I'm sorry to disturb you fellas and I realise that I'm as welcome here as a skunk in a French perfume factory," I whispered with a tinge of guilt at my intrusion into their lives, "but I'm not going anywhere in a hurry, even if you become as irate as a swarm of jitterbugging jellyfish with their tentacles in a tangle." The birds' stare of displeasure continued as though they'd understood every word then, resigned to the inevitability of my presence, they resumed their feast of nectar. Clinging tenaciously to slender twigs and golden blooms that were at the mercy of an increasing wind and swinging wildly to and fro, the tiny birds were seemingly unperturbed and even enjoying the ride.

White-plumed Honeyeaters, when quietly feeding alone or with a mate, appear to be meek and mild little characters, their soft chirping voices almost unheard above other sounds of the bush. But in the face of danger, such as that posed by a raptor or a reptile that may be intent on stealing eggs or chicks from a nest, or when other birds invade their territory and threaten to commandeer their sources of food, they utter a shrill call that summons their mates and with safety in numbers and demonstrating an unexpectedly aggressive side of their personality they gang up on the enemy and let intruders know that White-plumed Honeyeaters rule the roost in their neck of the woods.

Where you'll find them: They inhabit forests and woodlands that are close to waterways or wetlands. This species is found throughout mainland Australia, except in the tropical north, in the far south-west, and in the most arid inland regions.

Yellow-tufted Honeyeater

Lichenostomus melanops

On a meandering route to the Snowy Mountains I camped for the night beside the diminutive Badja River near the tiny New South Wales town of Numeralla. I'm usually up early every morning with bubbling enthusiasm to discover the creatures with which I'm sharing each unique environment, but this wasn't a normal morning for someone accustomed to a subtropical climate. With the temperature at an icy -6°C, icicles, formed from the moisture of my shivering breathe, hung from the ceiling of my campervan. The water that had been left overnight in a cup had turned to ice and frozen toothpaste refused to be squeezed from its tube. I questioned the sanity of crawling out of my warm sleeping bag before the sun had begun to melt the earth's carpet of glittering frost, but insanity ultimately won the conflict. Well rugged up and with only my face exposed to the biting cold, I wandered along the riverbank in search of any wild creatures that might be equally deranged and equally early risers.

There was plenty of evidence that wombats had wandered through the bushland's tangled vegetation during the night but with little other sign of wildlife I retreated back to my campsite. As magpies pleaded for me to offer them a few scraps of food I lit a small fire to keep the worst of the cold at bay and waited to see what other birds would share the morning. Crimson Rosellas were the first to appear, followed by Galahs and eventually I felt warm enough to venture more than a short distance from the fire.

I headed off along the riverbank, among low shrubs that rose in the shadows of lofty gum trees and it wasn't long before I spotted a small grey bird on a high branch. Before I could identify it, it was chased away by a Yellow-tufted Honeyeater that appeared from nowhere and vanished almost as quickly as it had unexpectedly appeared.

A couple of weeks later, on a contorted mountain trail near the New South Wales town of Bombala, where a diminutive stream severed the forest and brought a hint of light into the darkness, I discovered the perfect spot not only to stop for a picnic lunch but also to look for birds and I didn't have to wait long for some company to arrive. First on the scene was a White-faced Heron that paraded through the creek's shallow and rocky pools. A swarm of Bell Miners arrived too and as I watched their hyperactive antics a pair of Yellow-tufted Honeyeaters settled onto the twigs of a dead shrub at the water's edge.

These are birds that usually forage in the high canopy of forests and woodlands, plucking insects and other invertebrates from among the foliage, sipping nectar from delicate blooms and feasting on the sugary manna that oozes from the branches of some eucalyptus trees, but even they have to come down to the water sometimes.

"I'd hate to think that you were dirty birds," I whispered as, from my far-from-comfortable seat on a rock, I waiting patiently for the birds to overcome their timidity and flutter down to the water and get on with the serious business of bathing. One and then the other cautiously did what they'd come to do, keeping a wary on eye on their surroundings, on the heron and on me.

Yellow-tufted Honeyeaters are monogamous, with a pair spending their entire lives together in the same territory. After an all-too-brief encounter they retreated back to the treetops and I made a mental note to return to the area another day when these glorious golden birds, or their descendants, might thrill me with their beauty once again.

Where you'll find them: They inhabit eucalypt forests and woodlands in eastern and south-eastern regions of mainland Australia, with their extensive range extending from central Queensland to south-western Victoria and south-eastern South Australia.

OTHER PASSERINES

Passerines are a group of birds that are distinguished by the arrangement of their toes, with three pointing forward and one back, and that have tendons in their legs that tighten when the leg bends, causing the foot to curl and clamp onto a perch so that the bird can sleep without falling off.

Brown Treecreeper

Climacteris picumnus

As I sat quietly on the bank of a waterhole at Queensland's Culgoa Floodplain National Park there was little activity in this remote corner of the outback. A long and savage drought had take a cruel toll on the landscape, leaving the ground without a solitary blade of grass. A few murky waterholes were all that was left of a creek that, in better times, would be a picturesque and meandering stream.

I was confident that any wild creatures that had survived the punishing climatic conditions would eventually arrive to quench their thirst but at mid-afternoon the only creatures that were out and about were flies that, as they buzzed around my face and inspected every orifice, were as welcome as a sabre-toothed tiger at a pussy cats' ball.

"Do you want a cuppa?" my husband called from where he'd been having 40 winks in the shade of our campervan. "I'll be right there," I replied and it was then, as I moved from my seat on a waterfront log, that I glimpsed the first hint of action as a Brown Treecreeper peered cautiously around the trunk of a tree to see what all the commotion was about.

When I returned to my shaded birdwatching spot, with an ample supply of tea and biscuits, the bird appeared to have vanished from sight and it wasn't until it made a hesitant movement that its near-perfect camouflage was compromised. No one could be blamed for assuming that a Brown Treecreeper would simply creep around in trees all day long but this charming little character does far more than that. It's a bird that has no trouble coping with solitude but it had no complaints when a small group of its mates arrived on the scene and the cheerful and energetic little flock demonstrated that they're quite adept at doing more than merely tiptoeing around in trees.

They enthusiastically rummaged among fallen leaves beneath the eucalyptus trees and low shrubs that hemmed the remnants of the creek, snatching an insect here and another there and, as they hopped around my feet, I did my best imitation of a marble angel in a deserted desert graveyard, making little more than microscopic movements of my head as my eyes attempted to follow their energetic hunt for food. "Another cuppa luv?" my other half suddenly asked, using a whispering voice and subtle hand signals to avoid alarming my feathered friends. "I'd love one," I replied as quietly as I could, "but I'll have to wait until this cheerful little mob has moved elsewhere or I might step on them."

As dusk inevitably signalled that the end of the day was nigh, the night shift arrived on the scene and as kangaroos emerged from the woodlands and bounded towards the waterhole the Brown Treecreepers, with subtle twittering and expressions of consternation passing among the members of the little group, opted to move out of the way of the approaching mob. "We'd better head for our favourite roosting site before it's too dark to find our way," I'm sure I heard them murmur as they made a hasty retreat before the curtain of night was drawn across the landscape.

The next day, with impatience to discover which of my wild neighbours would be up and about

at the crack of dawn, I slithered out of my sleeping bag as the first rays of sunlight let the night know that its shift was over.

A rhythmic thud, thud, thud across the hard and barren outback soil was all the evidence I needed to know that the kangaroos were heading to the creek to start their day with a drink from the muddy water. As I settled down, with a slab of bread that would be the first simple course of my breakfast, the sun smiled through a fracture in the night's rapidly retreating clouds and the Brown Treecreepers fluttered to the ground and said "Good morning" with their cheerful twittering.

"It's about time you showed me your best party trick again," I demanded as the birds meandered among the fallen twigs and leaves that littered the ground. An obliging bird that glanced my way seemed to politely enquire "Is this what you want me to do?" as it crept around the weathered trunk of a nearby tree, progressing slowly upwards in an endless spiralling fashion that allowed the diminutive predator to inspect every inch of the tree's bark in its hunt for food. It pecked at an unseen insect here and another there, using its curved bill to extract other tasty morsels from the deepest recesses of the tree's bark and with ants being its favourite food a lot of pecking time would be required to keep hunger at bay.

Where you'll find them: They inhabit open woodlands that are dominated by eucalypts and that generally don't have a dense understorey of vegetation. Their extensive range stretches from the Cape York Peninsula in northern Queensland south to New South Wales and Victoria and to the Port Augusta and Flinders Ranges regions of South Australia.

Eastern Yellow Robin

Eopsaltria australis

When I arrived at Kings Plains National Park in New South Wales on a winter's morning the forest stage was set for some enthralling entertainment and a group of colourful performers took no time in welcoming me with their amusing antics. A large group of Eastern Yellow Robins, flitting here and there among the trees and low vegetation, seemed to be playing a game of hide and seek, inquisitively peering around the trunk of almost every tree. "Now you see me, now you don't," every bird grinned mischievously as it momentarily glanced in my direction then

disappeared – but while I was making a feeble attempt to hide from sight in the forest's dappled shadows it was the birds that were doing the seeking. They were hunting for their prey, using a well-honed technique that utilises patience, speed and the element of surprise and their continual success made the game look easy.

This attractive robin, in its distinctive pose, clings to the trunk of a tree from where it has an unimpeded view of the ground and of the comings and goings of any creatures that might provide a tasty snack. When its unsuspecting prey appears, the robin pounces with astounding speed and accuracy, scoffs its tiny victim and returns to its lookout position to wait for the next course on the menu to meander past. With spiders and insects such as moths, grasshoppers, ants, wasps and flies all forming part of its diet, variety is definitely the spice of life for these beautiful birds.

My next glimpse of an Eastern Yellow Robin was merely a flash of yellow that momentarily illuminated the shadows as the bird dashed through the forests of the Wollemi National Park in New South Wales as a deluge of rain inundated the landscape. For a moment I thought my eyes had deceived me but then I spotted the robin – a sodden little bundle of golden feathers – in his iconic pose as he scanned the saturated ground for any tiny creatures that might have been flushed from their subterranean retreats or washed from grasses and foliage by the splatter of heavy raindrops.

Eastern Yellow Robins live alone, with a mate, or as a member of a small family group. The next day, with the rain having retreated, Mister and Missus Robin proudly paraded before me with their gang of fledglings in tow and I watched with admiration as they gave their offspring a lesson in the skills of hunting. "Now watch what I do. You start like this," one parent seemed to be saying as it peered around the edge of a tree trunk with its gaze focused on the young birds that watched in awe as the maestro leapt to the ground. "Go on! You can do it! Give it a try!" I whispered as I waited and hoped to see the youngsters practice the skills they'd need to survive, but they were taking the easy option and foraging among fallen leaves and grasses until a family of Red-necked Wallabies bounded onto the scene and sent the little family darting back into the safety of the forest.

In recent years, as the undergrowth in the rainforest and woodland sections of my extensive garden have grown more dense, Eastern Yellow Robins have decided that this is the perfect place to call home on a permanent basis. They're unquestionably beautiful birds but I have to admit that that on more than one occasion I've cursed their presence and would have been pleased to see the back of the noisy little blighters. *Eopsaltria*, the name of the genus to which this species belongs, is an ancient word that means 'singer of the dawn' and it's a very appropriate title for the Eastern Yellow Robin is invariably the first bird to welcome each new day and the last to bid it farewell, with its chirping continuing well after dark.

This glamorous robin is no famed songbird but I'm happy to hear its voice when I'm out in the garden and I don't even complain too vociferously if, when I need to be up early, one takes on the role of nature's alarm clock. Well before the sun has yawned into life to greet a new day the robin begins its monotonous song that consists of nothing more than five or six high-pitched beeps, and when I'm sleeping soundly I sometimes hear the bird's repetitive call, *Beep, beep, beep, beep, beep.* "Can't you occasionally take a day off, or at least sleep in a little longer," I mumble with frustration as I stumble out of bed while my corner of the world is still enveloped in darkness.

The singer of the dawn is the early bird that gets the worm and at dusk, when other birds have settled down to roost, it is the last bird to take a dip in its favourite bird bath and the last avian voice to be heard before the night shift of owls and other nocturnal creatures come awake.

It has had no hesitation in claiming my garden as its personal domain and once, during my absence, a pair of Eastern Yellow Robins built their nest and raised a family in a hanging lampshade on the patio. There's nothing like making yourself at home, and who would really complain when such lovely creatures opt to share their environment?

Where you'll find them: These robins are residents of eastern mainland Australia with their range including coastal and adjacent hinterland areas from northern Queensland to the eastern section of South Australia. Their habitat includes eucalypt woodlands and rainforests, mallee and Acacia scrub and coastal heathlands, with urban parks and gardens that include suitable environments also tempting these attractive birds to make themselves at home.

Red-browed Finch

Neochmia temporalis

Only someone with the intelligence of a mouldy cheese sandwich would fail to comprehend the logic behind the common name of this attractive small bird, for its vivid red brow is there for all to see, as is its bright red bill and its red rump. My earliest encounter with a small flock of these hyperactive little finches was near the New South Wales coastal town of South West Rocks where

they were flitting among the grasses and other low vegetation that cloaked the sand dunes and they were here one minute and gone the next.

I met them once again when, in early summer, I was camping on the forested banks of the Connors River near the central Queensland town of Marlborough. Incessant and muted twittering was the first clue that a flock of Red-browed Finches was in the vicinity and as I homed in on the origin of the sound I discovered the little birds cavorting, in the company of Crimson Finches and Chestnut Manikins, in the shallow water at the river's edge.

"It's perfect weather and the perfect spot for a paddle," I whispered to the birds as, rather than have a swim as I'd intended, I settled down on the bank to watch the frenetic activity. Red-browed Finches are among Australia's smallest birds, yet they had no hesitation in getting up to their necks in the water as they ensured, with the vigorous flapping of their wings, that every feather was saturated and that every feather was spotlessly clean. When that objective had been achieved, it seemed that the only purpose of their activities was to have some fun as they frolicked with their mates, seeing who could make the greatest splash and who could create the highest sprays of water as every bird leapt and dived again and again into the cool clear stream.

A few years ago, when drought had battered the landscape with its iron fist, Red-browed Finches discovered a welcoming habitat in my forested garden and were obviously appreciative of the fact that food and water were available here even during the most punishing of seasons. "Now that you've found this wonderful place I hope you'll stay and raise a family here," I said quietly as I welcomed the new arrivals. They have graciously accepted my invitation and every year their population increases.

They're gregarious little birds that enjoy the company of their mates and certainly know how to have a good time. They bathe and play in the garden's ponds and bird baths, preen themselves in winter sunshine and summer shade and feast on the abundance of seeds provided by the grasses that are allowed to flourish in areas of the garden that never see a lawn mower. When I see them feeding I sit on the nearest garden bench to watch them, tiptoe discreetly past, or detour along an alternative route through the forest so I don't disturb them, but if these vigilant little birds spot me when I've wandered too close there's a panicked chorus of chirping followed by a flurry of wings and suddenly they vanish into the dense vegetation where they're as inconspicuous as a solitary fleck of dandruff in an aging celebrity's perfectly groomed hair.

In recent decades populations of Red-browed Finches have declined or disappeared entirely from rural areas that have been cultivated, heavily grazed by livestock, or suffered from the impact of long-term droughts, for in these situations the grass seeds that are their major source of food are either in short supply or non-existent, but in the forests of my garden there's always a banquet on offer to ensure that these admirable little birds can be as happy as a swarm of huntsman spiders at a cockroaches' convention.

Where you'll find them: They are found in eastern Australia, primarily on the coastal side of the Great Dividing Range, in an area that stretches from the northern tip of Queensland to eastern parts of South Australia. Their favoured habitats are open areas of tall grasses that are in close proximity to forests or dense woodlands yet not too far from water.

Red-capped Robin
Petroica goodenovii

I appreciate solitude and when, in the midst of winter, I was camping alone in Gundabooka National Park, south of the New South Wales outback town of Bourke, I had no concerns about either the remote location or the fact that there was no hint of the existence of any other human being.

It had been a night during which the silence had been fractured by nothing more than the sound of my tent flapping aimlessly in a subtle breeze and at dawn, as I munched on a simple breakfast and warmed myself beside a small fire, there was no more noise emanating from the landscape that was dominated by mulga trees and low shrubs, than you'd expect to hear at a termites' demolition party in a derelict outback shack.

"It's time I was off to meet the wild creatures of the bush," I muttered to myself as I snuffed out the last glowing embers of the fire that spat and sizzled in defiance as their heat turned water to steam and smouldering logs let out their last gasp of smoke.

"Were you looking for me?" a little voice chirped as a male Red-capped Robin magically appeared through the rapidly dissipating cloud of smoke like a genie emerging from a bottle. "Well here I am and aren't I gorgeous," he seemed to say as he twittered, danced and fluttered around on the weathered stump that he'd claimed as the stage for his brief impromptu performance. "I'm pleased to make your acquaintance Mister Robin," I whispered as I pulled on my jacket, slipped on my backpack with its supply of food and water and grabbed my camera. "It's time I was on my way but perhaps I'll see you again later," I said to the bird as I headed off along a faint track that speared into the dense bushland vegetation, but when I turned around to say goodbye the robin was nowhere to be seen.

Much later, I detoured from the meandering trail to look at some unfamiliar plants and to admire some tiny wildflowers. Suddenly I realised that, after having turned around and around in the mulga scrub, I had no idea where the path that would lead me back to my campsite lay and with clouds blanketing the sky I was unable to see the sun that might offer a clue as to which direction to take. I searched for any recognisable natural features that I'd passed on my way into the heart of the bushland, for fallen logs that I'd stepped over, for termite mounds and for fire-scarred trees, but with minimal variation in the vegetation panic descended momentarily as

I contemplated spending a night, or even longer, lost in the wilderness – alone – but I wasn't alone at all, for help was at hand.

"I'm so pleased to see you again," I said with a sigh of relief as a Red-capped Robin suddenly fluttered through the foliage, darting frenetically back and forth among the trees as though beckoning me to follow him in the opposite direction to the one that I had assumed would lead me back to the trail. I hesitantly followed my little saviour and in a few minutes miraculously stumbled across the track. Before I could say "Thanks for your assistance mate," the little bird had vanished as quickly and as silently as it had appeared.

I'm no stranger to arid landscapes and was visiting Lake Everard Station, a vast and remote sheep-grazing property in northern South Australia, during a time of severe drought. It was a grim time when every dam was dry, there was no hint of grass, no livestock and the only kangaroos on the barren plains were those that had died of starvation or thirst. It was a depressing situation but my husband and I had arrived at the ruins of an old cottage on one of the property's isolated outstations to celebrate better days, to celebrate the anniversary of his proposal of marriage. When he had worked on the property the now-derelict cottage had been his simple yet cosy home and

I had been a young girl making my first visit to the outback. We've survived many years of marriage and in this desolate yet beautiful location I encountered another great survivor, for it was here that I once again met a Red-capped Robin that, like others of his species, had thrived in what appears to be an incredibly hostile environment.

We've got a lot in common, this lovely robin and I and one characteristic that we share is our appreciation of solitude. Like me, he's often out in the bush on his own. Like me, he appreciates the company of his mate, and like me, he's definitely not a gregarious character and is never one to be seen in a crowd.

"Life must be tough out here mate but hopefully good rains will come soon to make life a little easier," I whispered as the little bird gazed at me from his perch on a tilting gate post. He seemed to nod in silent agreement as he fluttered down to rummage for food among a profusion of saltbush, one of the great survivors of the plant world that had replaced the floral shrubs that were once the focus of a well-tended cottage garden.

Red-capped Robins are skilful and agile hunters and although they occasionally catch their prey while in flight or while rummaging among the foliage of trees and shrubs, they generally utilise a less strenuous tactic. From a vantage point they pounce onto an unsuspecting victim as quickly as words of anger are vanquished by a smile and it's insects that are the robin's prey. Grasshoppers, moths and even bees provide tasty snacks for these tiny birds but a study of their dining habits has revealed that 95 per cent of their food consists of beetles, with most of the remainder being ants.

As my husband and I enjoyed a cuppa and reminisced about days long gone we watched the Red-capped Robin return to his perch to serenade us with his repetitious song. "Meeting you has been a pleasure sir," I whispered to the little performer, "So ta very much for the memory of another pleasurable outback encounter."

Where you'll find them: They inhabit arid and semi-arid regions of the Australian mainland, that lie to the west of the Great Dividing Range. Their favoured habitats are open woodlands dominated by Mulga, Eucalyptus or Cypress Pine trees.

Satin Bowerbird

Ptilonorhynchus violaceus

An adult male Satin Bowerbird wears no gaudy attire, but to say that he's dressed entirely in black is an understatement as pronounced as describing rubies as being merely red, for his glossy black plumage gleams with a deep blue metallic sheen. Juvenile males and females have a dramatically different appearance however, and although they wear primarily olive-green feathers the intricate patterns that decorate their plumage mean that they too are far from drab and unappealing characters.

It's the male bird's curious behaviour, rather than his appearance, that has brought this distinctive bird to prominence however, for he's one of the truly weird and wonderful creatures of the Australian bush and has a curious habit of collecting anything that's blue and that's small enough for him to carry to the secluded heart of his kingdom.

The sprawling picnic area at Queen Mary Falls, near the southern Queensland town of Warwick, is a regular haunt of Satin Bowerbirds that live in the surrounding forests. Although their natural foods include fruit, flowers, leaves, seeds and insects, they make regular forays into the open to enjoy any scraps of bread or other food that have been left by visitors. On the day that I visited the area, persistent rain put a damper on the activities of both myself and the birds.

Male Satin Bowerbirds are decidedly anti-social and reclusive characters that, except when mating, prefer their own company. It's only females and their immature male lookalikes that hang out together in small groups. As I stepped out of my vehicle I rushed through the rain to the shelter of one of the picnic area's covered tables, only to discover that a damp and rather dejected group of birds had adopted the same strategy to escape from the inclement weather. "Do you mind if I shelter here with you?" I asked in a quiet voice as the rain clattered down on the rusting tin roof. While most members of the little flock opted to escape to the seclusion of the forest rather than tolerate my company, one bird stoically remained on the table, staring me defiantly in the eye as if to say "I was here first and I'm not leaving for anyone!" "You really needn't worry about me, for I'll be as quiet as a cohort of dozing squid," I murmured. "All I want to do is to get out of the rain and admire your unparalleled beauty." The bird, beguiled by my flattery, happily posed for a few photos before eventually retreating to its natural habitat.

During the winter months male Satin Bowerbirds become obsessed with the task of constructing a bower. It's a relatively complex structure, for a bird, and the finished work of art is one that every male hopes will impress a harem of lovers. It consists of two parallel walls of vertical twigs, painted with a mixture of vegetable matter and saliva and that has a small clearing at each end. It's here that the proud owner of the bower displays every fragment of bling that he can find, from natural objects such as flowers and feathers to scraps of paper, plastic or metal, together with drinking straws and bottle tops. He's not fussy about the décor, providing everything is blue. To human eyes the completed bower might not look particularly inviting, but to a female bowerbird a well-decorated bower is as alluring as a pot of honey to a swarm of wasps.

The bower is where the male courts any female that wanders in to admire his handiwork and just to ensure that he gets her full attention he performs elaborate dances on his decorated 'stage'. If she's suitably impressed, the female enters the bower where the pair mate and once she's scurried away to begin the construction of her nest the male fastidiously rearranges his blue treasures in readiness to catch the eye of the next female that strolls his way.

Male Satin Bowerbirds are generally shy and reclusive characters but each bird's determination to create a highly ornate bower gives him the confidence he needs to pilfer the blue treasures that lie at the entrance of a competitor's bower and to scrounge around picnic and camping areas for anything blue that will enhance his creation. On more than one occasion a diligent bird has snatched a blue pen right from under my nose as I've worked at a picnic table that has become my temporary outdoor office.

My years of searching for a bower had yielded as much success as if I'd been on the hunt for a unicorn until I finally struck it lucky and discovered a bower in the most unexpected of places. One spring day, when the weather was in one of its most foul moods, I cancelled my plans to camp in a forest in Queensland's Sunshine Coast hinterland and grudgingly booked into a cabin

at a caravan park. A howling gale and torrential rain obliterated any thoughts of birdwatching but solitary confinement and isolation from the great outdoors left me feeling as irritable as a bunyip in a dried-up waterhole. I know myself well enough to realise that any attempt to stifle boredom is a task akin to trying to persuade a horde of rodents to sit still and listen to an entire AC/DC concert, so rather than face inevitable failure I grabbed an umbrella and ventured outside to explore the caravan park's extensive forested gardens.

A kookaburra, which had no option other than to face the inclement weather, was sitting on a fence post with water streaming across its feathers. The bedraggled bird glared at me and began its iconic cackling call as I squelched across a sodden lawn. "Only mad dogs and Englishmen go out in the midday rain," was the clear message that it seemed to convey. "You could be right mate," I said as I quietly responded to its unspoken words of derision, "and you wouldn't be the first to suggest that if I had two more brain cells I could qualify for the position of the village idiot."

As the rain intensified and the wind threatened to hurl my umbrella to kingdom come a fragment of blue among the shrubs of a garden bed caught my attention and there, on the doorstep of both the forest and suburbia, I discovered a Satin Bowerbird's bower, complete with its motley collection of blue adornments. The owner of the structure, like all intelligent creatures, had taken refuge from the storm and was nowhere to be seen.

Where you'll find them: In eastern Australia, from around Gladstone in central Queensland as far south as the Dandenong and Otway Ranges in Victoria, with smaller populations thriving in far north Queensland. They generally inhabit woodlands and damp forests but will also set up home in urban parks and gardens if these have the appropriate vegetation that will provide the birds with food. During winter months they tend to inhabit relatively open woodlands but when their thoughts are focused on finding a mate they return to the more congested growth of forests and each male enthusiastically begins preparing his territory to impress the females.

Spotted Bowerbird
Chlamydera maculata

As the only human in temporary residence at the Nymboi-Binderay National Park, near the New South Wales town of Dorrigo, I was confident that I'd share the environment with an abundance of birds, for the forests here are home to many stunning species, including Superb Lyrebird, Wompoo Fruit-Dove and Regent Bowerbird. As I warmed myself beside my campfire I unexpectedly slipped into the land of nod and dreamt of the wonderful creatures that I might discover in the days to come, but I came coughing and spluttering back to reality as a breeze blew a cloud of smoke from the dying fire in my direction. I added some more firewood and prodded the embers back into

action but as damp timber hissed and feeble flames reluctantly licked at smouldering wood another noise drew my attention away from the fire. It was a subtle noise that emanated from the margin of the forest where a Spotted Bowerbird, its mottled brown plumage ensuring that it was well camouflaged among the ebony shadows, rummaged among fallen leaves with as much concern about my presence as if I had been nothing more than a discarded and mouldy tea bag.

With its eyes scouring the ground and its feet scratching incessantly to turn every fragment of forest debris in its hunt for food, it dawdled past the fire and only became aware of my presence when I slowly reached for my camera. The bird looked up with an expression that could only be interpreted as saying "Where on earth did you come from? Well, that doesn't matter. You look harmless enough," and it continued on its way, flinging leaves and twigs into the air and prying among my kindling wood for any hint of a snack before ultimately wandering back into the seclusion of the forest.

Luck ensured that I was treated to a more impressive performance by a Spotted Bowerbird when I visited the Culgoa Floodplain National Park in outback Queensland. The landscape had been battered by a long and brutal drought and with pools of water as scarce as a scarecrow's tears I knew that if I waited long enough birds and other wild creatures would eventually flock to any small and murky pool of water that had survived the harsh climatic conditions.

"That's the perfect spot for lunch," I proclaimed as my husband drove our campervan past an isolated pool beside the meandering and dusty track. While my other half dutifully made a simple meal, I grabbed a chair to make myself comfortable on birdwatching duty in the shade of some scrawny Mulga trees and picked up my camera in case any bird should be foolish enough to be out in the midday sun. "Abracadabra, make some birds appear," I whispered as I made a dramatic magician's flourish with my arms and settled down for what I had assumed would be an interminable wait. But before I even had time to finish casting my spell, a Spotted Bowerbird appeared from nowhere and landed on a mound of dead vegetation that protruded from the muddy water.

After a quick sip of water the bird disappeared into the adjacent woodland as quickly and silently as it had arrived on the scene. "I'll have to work on creating a longer-lasting spell," I said as my husband arrived with a sandwich and some coffee. As I dined on the simplest of fare I continued to peer into the shadows of the woodlands hoping for another glimpse of this beautiful bird. Time and patience were once again the key ingredients for success that allowed me to watch the Spotted Bowerbird's secretive life. From the relative comfort of my camping chair I watched it rummaging on the ground for the fruits, flowers, seeds and insects that form the major part of its diet and wondered if it would eventually show me what else it did with its time, for it's not only the search for food that keeps Spotted Bowerbirds as busy as a swarm of wasps in a jam factory.

They have other important tasks that keep them occupied, with males of the species, like those of the more familiar Satin Bowerbird, being fanatical scavengers. Unlike their relatives that gather anything that's blue, the male of this species brings a touch of bling to his world. He enthusiastically gathers up anything that's either white or shiny and humans have provided him with an endless supply of stuff that takes his fancy. Silver foil food wrappers, shards of glass, aluminium bottle caps and ring pulls are all on the shopping list of this avian kleptomaniac and if he's given the opportunity to snatch a piece of sparkling jewellery he certainly won't refuse.

Every scrap of treasure is destined to enhance the decor of the avian scrounger's bower, a structure that consists of two parallel walls built from vertical sticks and grass and that has the sole purpose of attracting females with which the bird that's the king of the castle can mate. The clearings at each end of the bower, where the bird's gleaming objects lie scattered among an array of white pebbles and fragments of sun-bleached bones and shells, are where the male puts on an impassioned performance whenever a female wanders into view.

I was confident that somewhere, perhaps not far from where I sat, a bird would be performing an energetic dance, accompanied by a repertoire of curious calls, to impress his female audience – and whenever I encounter a Spotted Bowerbird and whatever it's doing, I'm inevitably impressed too.

Where you'll find them: They inhabit inland areas on the eastern side of the Australian mainland and thrive in dry woodlands west of the divide in Queensland and New South Wales.

Western Bowerbird

Ptilonorhynchus guttatus

My initial encounter with a Western Bowerbird was at an isolated camping area in the West MacDonnell Ranges of Central Australia, where the golden-brown bird was warming itself on a boulder in the mid-winter sunshine. "Turn around and let me take a good look at you," I pleaded in my most persuasive whispering voice and the little fella obligingly performed an elegant pirouette. That was enough to give me a glimpse of the vivid pink band that adult birds wear on the back of their neck – a feature that makes the Western Bowerbird instantly recognisable.

Suddenly a herd of vociferous campers stomped into view, hurrying on their way to a prominent tourist attraction with no concern about the natural wonder that was right under their noses. The bird made a panicked exit from the scene to find a more peaceful refuge among the adjacent woodland vegetation. That might be, I assumed, where his bower would be hidden, so I tiptoed after him as quietly and secretively as a caterpillar in a cabbage patch. The best option, if the bird hadn't scurried too far away, was simply to sit and wait, so I settled down on a log well away from any trail frequented by tourists who might come parading across the landscape and I began doing something at which every birdwatcher should be most proficient – waiting.

Eventually boredom set in and as the late afternoon breezes of an outback winter arrived with an icy touch I was ready to admit that the Western Bowerbird had eluded me. It was then that my husband appeared to enquire who would be cooking our evening meal. "And would you like your waiter to deliver it to you out here if you don't come back to the camping area?" he added with his usual touch of sarcasm. "Just give me five more minutes," I said with reluctance to leave the log to which my anatomy seemed to have become permanently welded. "I'm sure the bird will be back soon, and I just want one more glimpse of it."

It was then that I noticed the decaying native figs that were scattered across the ground. These are a delicacy that Western Bowerbirds find simply irresistible and I was confident that if my quarry realised that a banquet was on offer he or she would put in an appearance sooner rather than later.

Finally my patience was rewarded as a bird came energetically hop, hop, hopping across the stony ground, peering here and there, scratching among the leaf litter in its search for seeds or insects that would make a palatable snack. When it spotted the fallen fruit it looked as excited as a dog that thought it would dig up an old soup bone and found a dinosaur instead.

"Perhaps tomorrow you could show me where your bower is hidden," I whispered as the bird, oblivious to my presence, gorged itself. Each male Western Bowerbird, like other species of bowerbirds, attracts a series of mates by constructing a bower. To enhance his creation, which is an avenue of sticks and grass stems, he fanatically collects a horde of treasures that are primarily white or green and that include bleached fragments of bone, shells, seed pods, stones and scraps of plastic. With the decor of his bower displayed to perfection the male begins an energetic dance, twirling around, flicking his wings and proudly raising his small bright pink crest of feathers. What passing female could resist such an amorous and good-looking fella?

Where you'll find them: These bowerbirds inhabit open woodlands and thickets of shrubs that are generally in rocky gorges and rugged ranges in arid inland regions of central Australia and semi-arid regions of Western Australia.

Superb Fairy-wren

Malurus cyaneus

It might be hard to believe that anyone could ever resent the presence of Superb Fairy-wrens, but these attractive little birds have perfected the art of making a nuisance of themselves. It was during a bitterly cold winter, while I was camping among the forests of the Wollemi National Park in New South Wales, that I first made the acquaintance of these hyperactive characters. With no other humans in the vicinity, they invited themselves to become my companions for several days and insisted on commandeering the picnic table as the focus of their activities. Every lunchtime they hopped across my sandwiches and scoffed as many crumbs as they could before I shooed them away. And they bathed in the bowl of washing-up water in which I'd lazily left my crockery and saucepans soaking, with their little wings stirring a hint of detergent into billowing foam as

they seemed more intent on having fun than in the serious business of cleaning their plumage.

The inquisitive little blighters fluttered around inside my tent, clambered into my sleeping bag and explored the heap of dirty clothes that, being a temporary slob when camping, I'd tossed into a corner of my humble abode. When I moved the birds on yet again they fluttered so close to my campfire that I expected to see one or more of them with singed feathers and blistered toes. As I boiled some water on my stove they scampered around my feet, forcing me to keep one eye on the pot of bubbling stew and one eye on the ground to ensure that I didn't tread on a fairy-wren or two.

The highlight of one day came when I was entertained by the hyperactive little birds as they took turns sliding down the handle of a spatula that had been left outside overnight and that was frozen into the ice that was once the water in my washing up bowl. I couldn't contain my laughter as I watched their tiny faces and heard their incessant twittering that I interpreted as an avian version of "Whoopee!" "What fun you lot are having," I said, not bothering to whisper as there seemed to be no possibility that something as simple as a few words would disrupt their pleasure and frighten them away.

If Superb Fairy-wrens could be assigned human characteristics, friendly, cheeky, mischievous and extroverted would all be quite appropriate. These charismatic and inquisitive little birds are tenacious creatures too and the stubborn determination of one individual was on display at the Wallingat National Park in New South Wales. I'd enjoyed a day of fine weather but on day two of my stay in this densely forested park the weather gods were not on my side and I had no option other than to spend the day sitting under the awning of my tent watching the landscape receive a drenching. Few birds were out and about, not that I could blame them but on that day, when there had been as much activity from both wildlife and humans as there might be at an annual gathering of barnacles. I became excited as noon approached. It was the anticipation of the highlight of the day's activities that got my blood pumping, anticipation of an event that would be only a tad more exciting than watching a game of cricket in slow motion. It was time to make lunch and boil the kettle for a cuppa but as I tried to decide what item on my limited culinary repertoire would top

the menu, along came Mister Fairy-wren and food was on his mind too.

Ignoring the rain, he waded through puddles, fluttered among grasses that were bent down under the weight of raindrops and pecked at the muddy ground – then suddenly he hit the jackpot. He began pulling up an earthworm that, in relation to a fairy-wren, was a gigantic creature. I watched the battle of bird against worm in silent awe as the fairy-wren demonstrated the tenacity of a pet rat on a treadmill and the worm equally stubbornly refused to submit to a fate that could only result in its death. It stood little chance of survival however, for in the sodden ground and with a determined enemy it would either drown or be eaten, neither being a good option from a worm's perspective. The bird was the ultimate victor, cramming the worm that was longer than its entire body into its bill, one juicy bit after another.

The bird stood in the rain, savouring the reward of its efforts. "Now you've got a full stomach perhaps it's time to find somewhere to shelter from the rain," I quietly suggested as the wren appeared unsure what to do next. Then suddenly it made a decision and took my advice – and fluttered into my tent. "Why don't you make yourself at home," I said sarcastically, "but don't burn your feet on the hot kettle," I added as it landed on the table to inspect my food. As it settled onto the book that I'd been reading and began to preen its saturated feathers, I didn't have the heart to shoo it out into the cold and miserable weather.

Over the years I've had numerous delightful encounters with Superb Fairy-wrens that live in small family groups. I've been mesmerised by every glimpse into their lives as I've watched them flitting among tall grasses and dense shrubs in their usual hyperactive way as they search for insects that are the main component of their diet that also includes seeds, small flowers and of course earthworms.

Although it's usually a gaudy male that's the first to capture my attention I never ignore the females of the species, even though they're far less glamorous than their companions. During the breeding season the male, with his iridescent blue plumage, is as conspicuous as a shark in a goldfish bowl, but it's only males that are more than four years of age that retain their gaudy plumage all year long. The younger little blokes and females have drab brown plumage but with all males having dark blue tails and females wearing an orange patch around each eye there's no confusion about who's who in the wonderful world of Superb Fairy-wrens.

Where you'll find them: They inhabit woodland areas that have dense undergrowth, grasslands with scattered low shrubs, and thickets of lantana and blackberries within south-eastern Queensland, New South Wales, Victoria, the south-eastern corner of South Australia and Tasmania.

White-browed Scrubwren

Sericornis frontalis

I've seen White-browed Scrubwrens on many occasions when I've been camping in the bush and despite their diminutive stature and their far-from-gaudy plumage these charismatic little characters, that are invariably as conspicuous as a herd of dancing hippos in purple tutus, deserve an award for being the most entertaining of birds. They twitter incessantly as they flutter among low vegetation and feed on insects and the seeds of grasses, but in the Nymboi-Binderay National Park, near the New South Wales town of Dorrigo, one of these endearing little birds was impossible to ignore when it invited itself into my campervan. It peered into my sleeping bag, discovered crumbs in the kitchen sink and inspected an open drawer for any hint of other food, but finding it as bare as old Mother Hubbard's cupboard the little intruder gave me a stern glare of displeasure as it fluttered past on its way back to the outside world.

"You could have left a little bit of cake or something else for me to eat!" its twittering voice seemed to say and I knew that wouldn't be the last I'd see of this extroverted little character.

The next morning I was up and about before the first rays of the morning sun had chased away the night and as the temperature struggled to rise above zero I lit a small fire to keep the winter's cold at bay, but I wasn't the only one appreciating a little warmth. I turned my back on the flames for only a few seconds but that was long enough for two White-browed Scrubwrens to move in

to warm their little feet on the rocks beside the fire. "I've got no magical cure for singed toes and smouldering feathers, so you'd better keep a bit further away from the flames if you know what's good for you," I said as the birds acknowledged my presence with nothing more than a perplexed stare that let me know that my words of concern for their wellbeing would be as effective as demanding, with a few persuasive words, that the ocean's encroaching tide should cease its advance onto the shore.

Eventually they hopped across to my heap of firewood, pecking at tiny insects that they discovered, before fluttering onto the picnic table where I'd left an inviting slice of bread. With the table white with frost the little birds slithered rather than hopped across the surface and stumbled over the plate of bread before colliding with a cup and, as they skated towards the table's edge, they glared at me with a scowl that seemed to infer that, if they could speak, they'd lay the blame for the icy conditions on me. "I hope you enjoyed the winter sports fellas," I called after them as they retreated into the dense vegetation of the forest.

For me, there's no escape from White-browed Scrubwrens, for several years ago they discovered the pleasures of life in my forested garden and it seems that they're here to stay. I'm well aware when they're in the vicinity for these hyperactive little chatterboxes always have a lot to say. I watch them cavorting in their favourite bird bath, spraying water high into the air before, with incessant twittering and chirping, they retreat to the dense foliage of a nearby wattle tree to preen their feathers. Every day I see them flying here, there and everywhere among the garden's chaos of vegetation and I keep my fingers crossed that they and I won't be on a collision course as they zoom around the patio and dash into my office whenever the door leading to the garden is open. Where their rambling flights of adventure will lead is something that's as unpredictable as the journey of a solitary feather in a fan factory, with the only certainty being their arrival at the window of my office, for every day scrubwrens come tap, tap, tapping on the glass as they conceitedly admire their reflections.

Life is generally easy for the small flock of birds that have claimed my garden as their personal kingdom but I have to admit that, on one occasion, my actions played havoc with their plans. One spring morning, as I was weeding a garden bed, I noticed a tangled mass of dead leaves and cobwebs among the large and spiny foliage of a clump of bromeliads. I assumed that it was nothing more than debris that had fallen from the overhanging trees but I realised my mistake the moment I'd pulled the matted vegetation out and tossed it into the wheelbarrow. I had destroyed the nest of a White-browed Scrubwren.

Guilt slowly washed over me like a flood of mercury but I salved my conscience with the fact that the nest was still a work in progress and contained neither eggs nor chicks. When a bird arrived with strands of cobweb to add to her tangled creation she gazed in dismay at the destruction I'd wrought. "What can I say other than sorry," I mumbled with embarrassment, "but you'd have to admit that distinguishing between your untidy nest and a heap of rubbish really is almost as impossible as spotting the difference between two weevils in a sack of rice." The little bird looked at me with a perplexed expression but I hoped I'd be forgiven and that the birds would eventually rebuild their nest and raise a family elsewhere in the garden.

A few days later, while I was working among a chaos of shrubs, a White-browed Scrubwren rushed past with a caterpillar in its bill and as a convoy of birds followed, each bearing a gift

of a grasshopper or a wriggling grub, it was obvious that the birds were again in the family way and that somewhere nearby young birds were demanding food. It was only a matter of time before I spotted a ramshackle nest among a cluster of ferns. With the nest being almost on the ground any chicks would be vulnerable to predation by cats, foxes and reptiles but the tiny face that peered out at me was too young and innocent to have any concept of fear or of the thin line dividing life from death.

White-browed Scrubwrens live in small family groups with every bird helping to feed and rear their young. Over the following days I watched their frenetic activity as they attempted to satisfy the chicks' insatiable appetite but one morning I arrived to find the nest empty and not a solitary scrubwren in sight. Sadness engulfed me as I entertained pessimistic visions of the fate of the young birds, but the following day my fears were dispelled and I was reminded that scrubwrens are birds that are as invincible as a freedom fighter's enduring dream of peace.

As I was watering some plants outside my office window a bird, with a caterpillar in its bill, zoomed past my head and landed on the window sill, jumping up and down and fluttering frantically as it tapped incessantly on the glass. "I've always assumed that your mob are a little bit on the crazy side of doolally but if you're trying to feed your reflection then you've really lost the plot," I said as I watched the bird's antics but I had to retract my words of derision when I realised that the bird was attempting to reach a chick that, on its first adventure beyond the nest, had flown into my office.

I gently picked up the tiny bird that sat quietly on my hand as I carried it outside. "That's enough adventure for you my lad," I whispered to the fragile creature that stared in amazement at the first human that it had ever encountered. "It's time to enjoy life in the great outdoors," I said but it seemed in no hurry to leave and simply squatted down in my cupped hand as though it had found the perfect comfort blanket. Suddenly Mrs Scrubwren arrived on the scene, fluttering silently down onto a branch of a nearby shrub with her offering of food still firmly grasped in her bill and the young bird, with a feeble chirp, the avian equivalent of "Mummy! Mummy!" flew off to begin its life in the wilds of the garden.

From that moment every White-browed Scrubwren disappeared from sight and although I wasn't sorry to see the back of them, I was overjoyed when, several days later, they returned to the garden once again, for although these perpetually cheerful birds with their vibrant personalities have occasionally been annoying, the joy that they've brought to my life has been immeasurable and the pleasure of their company has cost no more than a breath of fresh air.

Where you'll find them: Their range includes a wide coastal strip that extends from northern Queensland through to South Australia and to the mid Western Australian coast. They are also found in coastal areas of Tasmania where their habitat, as on the mainland, includes forests and woodlands.

Willie Wagtail
Rhipidura leucophrys

I've see him here, I've see him there, I've see him almost everywhere, for the charismatic little Willie Wagtail, in his smart black-and-white uniform, is among the most common of birds – but common is not a word that carries any derogatory connotations as far as this endearing little character is concerned.

Mister William Wagtail has been my faithful companion for aeons and has accompanied me on every journey, or at least that's how it seems, for whenever I stop and step out of my vehicle during a trip into the bush or even into the most remote corner of the outback he's there to greet me. It's almost as though he's tucked himself into one of my campervan's many crevices or clung tenaciously onto the bull bar and hitched a ride to every destination. "I hope you enjoyed the journey and didn't get too windblown," I often greet him as he flutters joyfully before me, but his

monochrome plumage is invariably immaculate with not a single feather ruffled or flecked with dust.

I never need to be coy or cautious in my interactions with this perpetually joyful little fella for the Willie Wagtail, who entertains me with his cheerful twittering as he wags his tail rapidly from side to side, never has any intentions of disappearing from sight. It appears that his only aim is to please me and that's something that my mate William always does to perfection.

This is not a bird that makes himself unwelcome by continually scrounging for food, for he has no interest in breadcrumbs or any scraps

of the food that I find delicious. He's a skilful hunter that catches his own food and he likes nothing better than a feast of insects that, with astounding speed and agility, he grabs from the air while in flight.

A Willie Wagtail is a regular visitor to one of the bird baths in my forested garden but it was an enthralling outback performance by one of these personable little birds that became one of my most memorable avian encounters. On a journey through south-western Queensland I'd stopped to photograph a mob of kangaroos that were dozing in the dense shade of a cluster of Yapunyah trees and while I captured a portrait of the family group my other half had other things to do. As an insomniac he spends most nights awake and often needs to catch a nap during the day and when I returned to our campervan he was sleeping soundly. Rather than disturb him, I grabbed some cake and a flask of water, wandered across to a nearby waterhole and took up a birdwatching position on a log beneath the shading vegetation, but I wasn't alone, for Willie Wagtail had discreetly followed me.

"I'm sure you're not here simply to keep me company?" I whispered as the little bird settled on the ground beside me. "Wherever there's water there are sure to be plenty of insects, so you should be able to get plenty of tucker here," I informed young William. It was a fact that I'm sure he already knew and he glared at me with a look of amazement that momentarily left me feeling a tad embarrassed. "And you thought I didn't know that?" its stare seemed to say and little Willie Wagtail fluttered off to satisfy both its own desire for food and my unspoken demand for entertainment.

With its wings outstretched it danced above the murky water as elegantly as the most accomplished of ballerinas, with the grace of Margot Fonteyn and the strength and stamina of Rudolf Nureyev. It twirled and pirouetted tirelessly in a gracefully and perfectly choreographed performance. It banked from side to side, its wings momentarily dipping into the water and twirled around and around again and again. Finally Mister William Wagtail, in his slow and calculated finale, did a slow lap around the perimeter of the waterhole before settling on a rock

that protruded from the coffee-coloured soup and took a well-deserved bow before his awestruck audience of one, then took to the air once again for an encore performance.

"I'm sorry I left you on your own for so long," my husband said as he arrived on the scene, yawning and rubbing his eyes, yet refreshed after his midday nap. He hadn't noticed my little mate, the enchanting Willie Wagtail, who, with a facial expression that was nothing short of avian laughter, had settled quietly onto a nearby branch. "You must have been bored out here with nothing to do," my human mate said with genuine concern but I'm never bored when I'm in the bush and certainly not when I have my feathered friends to entertain me.

Aboriginal people are said to be wary of Willie Wagtails for they believe that the birds eavesdrop on their conversations and reveal their secrets to others. I have no such concerns for I harbour no secrets that I'm reluctant to share, not even the secret of my next outback destination. "I'll see you at the next stop," I call to the Willie Wagtail each time I clamber back into my vehicle and I know my little mate will be there to greet me once again.

Where you'll find them: They are found throughout mainland Australia in a wide range of habitats and are regular visitors to many urban parks and gardens.

Zebra Finch

Taeniopygia guttata

When I arrived in Australia as a child my mother promised to buy me a bird to replace the budgie that I had tearfully left behind. When my gift eventually arrived I excitedly removed the wrapping from the cage and my gaze of wonder was returned by the stare of one of Australia's smallest and most charismatic birds. *Pleased to meet you! Pleased to meet you!* the exuberant chirping voice of a Zebra Finch seemed to say as he jiggled about on his perch with an expression that could only be described as a joyous avian grin. "I'm very pleased to meet you too," I replied as I admired the beautiful bird with his colourful speckled plumage. Mister Speckie became his name and providing me with pleasure seemed to be his primary goal in life.

Eventually he was joined by Missus Speckie and although with her relatively dull fawn plumage she wasn't the most alluring of characters Mister Speckie certainly had no complaints about his new companion. The devoted lovebirds were the focus of my attentions for almost a year and when my father constructed an aviary that became their new home I was confident that I'd eventually hear the patter of little Speckie feet, but one day someone left the aviary door open and when morning came the birds had flown the coop. My initial sadness was replaced with delight when I spotted the tiny birds in a neighbour's garden and my sense of loss was banished by happiness as I watched the finches experiencing the joys of freedom before they vanished from sight as rapidly as an ice cube on a bonfire.

Zebra Finches are the most common and widespread of the several species of grass finches that call Australia home. I've often seen large flocks in the wild and when, one winter's afternoon, I stopped to photograph the varied species of birds that were taking advantage of an outback Queensland waterhole, I was optimistic that finches would also put in an appearance. I plonked my camping chair down on the bank of the waterhole in a spot where I'd be partially camouflaged by one of the few sparse shrubs that were dotted across the arid and stony landscape. My husband dutifully delivered a cup of coffee and a light snack and we sat together in silence in anticipation of other avian arrivals that would find the water in this arid region simply irresistible

Eventually my patience was rewarded as, one by one, a flock of Zebra Finches fluttered down to the water's edge with more continually arriving until there was barely room for a centipede to slither through the crowd. For a moment I fancifully imagined that these might be the descendants of Mister Speckie and his mate. "One wild bird in the bush is worth more than 1,000 kept captive in a cage and I hope you all appreciate the pleasures of freedom," I whispered as more and more birds continued to arrive.

One colourful little male confidently waded into the edge of the murky water to drink and bathe while a female, who would be his mate for life, waited nearby. "Come on in, darlin', the water's great," he chirped as he splashed exuberantly in the shallows. With tiny and hesitant steps Missus Speckie and other members of the flock eventually joined him.

Zebra Finches are so small that they're almost submerged by merely 5cm of water, but these courageous little characters dipped and dived and plunged their tiny heads and bodies beneath the coffee-coloured water, emerging with wings flapping wildly and showering others with water as the serious business of having a bath was replaced with the frivolity of simply having fun.

Gradually, one sodden bird after another, they flew to a cluster of shrubs that cast long afternoon shadows over the landscape and, with incessant chattering among the flock, they preened themselves meticulously. When every feather had been cleaned and perfectly arranged, they fluttered silently down to the ground to feed on an abundance of grass seeds.

A day dominated by communal fun in the water and a nutritious feast came to a close for the flock of Zebra Finches and I had no doubt that these hyperactive and gregarious little birds, with their perpetually cheerful personalities, would settle down for the night with less complaints about their life in the wild that a skulk of foxes might have after a night of feasting at a poultry farm. I'd loved Mister and Missus Speckie when they were confined within a cage but I would have had to be as blind as a slab of granite not to appreciated the charms of these appealing little finches in their natural habitat.

Where you'll find them: They are found throughout the Australian mainland, with the exception of the Cape York Peninsula in Queensland. Although they are most prominent in arid and semi-arid regions, they also inhabit some coastal areas.

Index